THE C.O.D.E.

Affirmations for Walking in the Jesus Way

Tom Johnston and Mike Chong Perkinson, with Marjorie L. Clark, John Kimball, Tim McGinnin Jr., Selina McGinnin, Deryk Richenburg, and Troy Sonnleitner

PraxisMedia

ISBN-13: 9780982272756
ISBN-10: 0982272758

Cover Design: Britney Bennett
Layout: Jodie McCay
Copy Editor: Marjorie Clark

Printed in the United States of America

CONTENTS

INTRODUCTION – PART 1

by Dr. Tom Johnston

Throughout the ages, Christian communities have embraced a "Rule of Life," or discipleship pattern, in order to walk with Jesus together in their life and mission. Here the word "rule" comes from the Latin regula and is where we get the word regulate, like a pendulum regulates a grandfather clock. Basically, it's a spiritual rhythm for life together in Christ. Regula is also the root word in Latin for thread, with the Rule of Life being a "common thread" for a community. By grabbing onto this thread, we are able to walk together in Christ and grow as a Kingdom community. The following "Rule of Life," or discipleship pattern, is intended to help us in our common pursuit of our life mission. This rule of life consists of the following three elements:

Affirmations from Scripture for daily reflection and prayer

Spiritual disciplines we will commit to embracing

Daily and weekly rhythms for engaging God in these disciplines

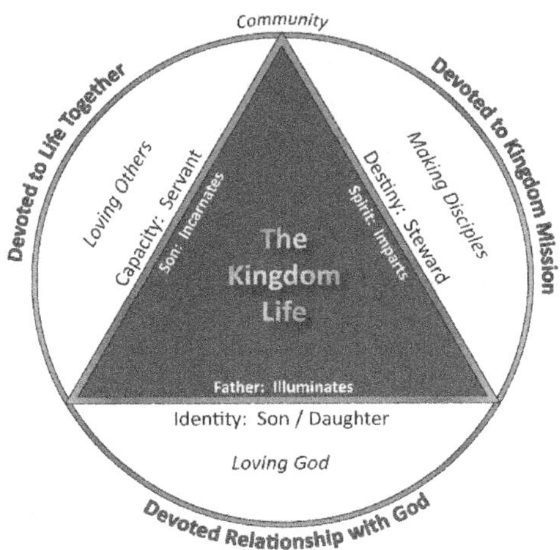

We call this Rule of Life the C.O.D.E. – *Christians Observing Disciplines Everyday*. It is also short-hand for "genetic code" – the basic building blocks of who we are as disciples of Jesus. It all flows from two summary passages of Scripture often referred to as The Great Commandments, and the Great Commission. Jesus is calling us into *a way of life,* going beyond simply believing in God to embracing His Lordship in our lives and receiving all the benefits of His Kingdom rule (Luke 4:16-21). Jesus made some very powerful summary statements about all of this, recorded in the Gospel of Matthew. First, in Matthew 22:34-40 it says—

> *But when the Pharisees heard that he had silenced the Sadducees, they gathered together. And one of them, a lawyer, asked him a question to test him. "Teacher, which is the great commandment in the Law?"*
>
> *And he said to him, "You shall love the Lord your God with all your heart and with all your soul and with all your mind. This is the great and first commandment. And a second is like it: You shall love your neighbor as yourself. On these two commandments depend all the Law and the Prophets."*

In answering the man's question, Jesus quotes from Deuteronomy 6:5 and Leviticus 19:18b, joining together the loving of God with our whole life and our loving of others. By saying "a second is like it," Jesus makes them of equal importance, indicating that one cannot truly love God if they do not have love for the people whom God has created. The man came to Jesus asking what the *greatest rule* was, and Jesus speaks instead of the commandments of God being about *two relationships*—our relationship with God and our relationships with others—all rooted in the love He has already shown **us (1 John 4:19). Indeed, we often call the passage** *The Great Commandments,* as it sums up what God is seeking in His people. In fact, in John 13:33-35, Jesus said He was giving all who followed Him a new commandment—

> *Little children, yet a little while I am with you. You will seek me, and just as I said to the Jews, so now I also say to you, 'Where I am going you cannot come.' A new commandment I give to you, that you love one another: just as I have loved you, you also are to love one another. By this all people will know that you are my disciples, if you have love for one another."*

Jesus told the Pharisee who came to him that all of the Hebrew scripture was summed up in these two things—*loving God with everything we are and loving and caring for our neighbor even as we would love and care for ourselves.* Everything the Lord God was trying to communicate to people was how we could be restored back into relationship with our Father in Heaven and with each other. That's good news! And that's what Jesus came to teach us as being central to the way of life He was calling us to—a way of love. These "Great Commandments" are the heart of all that Jesus wanted us to know and to live.

The second aspect of Jesus' call to His way of life was His commission to His followers, as they journeyed through life, to make more disciples, as we see in Matthew 28:18-20—

> *And Jesus came and said to them, "All authority in heaven and earth has been given to me. Go therefore and make disciples of all nations, baptizing them in the name*

> *of the Father and of the Son and of the Holy Spirit, teaching them to observe all that I have commanded you. And behold, I am with you always, to the end of the age."*

Jesus' instruction was that what He had commanded His followers to embrace, they were now to teach others how to do, so they too might come back into relationship with God and join the way of life Jesus had set out for us. Jesus commissioned these disciples to tell people about Him, share His teaching and to show people what following Him looks like—how to live the way of Jesus. The "go therefore" could be translated "in going from here" or "as you go from here" —basically, as you go through life, make disciples. Share the good news of Jesus, showing people how to live His *way of love* as their *way of life.* Christians often refer to this passage in Matthew 28 as *The Great Commission,* the sending forth of His disciples, which extends to all Christians even in our day. We believe we too are called to join Christ Jesus in His mission of seeing His Kingdom extended and more people reconciled with their Father, everywhere we go.

As we look at these two passages in Matthew, we see a summary of the life Jesus called us to—we are to love God with everything we are, to love others as we would ourselves and to make more disciples of Jesus as we go through life. The Great Commandments and the Great Commission are at the heart of the Jesus way. We refer to this as the "Irreducible Core of the Christian Life." We believe that you can do more than this, but we don't believe Jesus asks us to do less than this:

> *Love God with everything we are because He has loved us with everything He is,*
>
> *Love and serve others because He first loved us and*
>
> *Make disciples for Jesus as we live life, every day, everywhere we go.*

Ask yourself these questions:

How am I doing at living out the "Irreducible Core?" How am I doing at loving God? Loving and serving others? Making disciples for Jesus?

Pray this prayer:

Father God, thank You for Your Word and the instruction You give me through it. Holy Spirit, open both my heart and my mind to know and love God. Free my heart that I might love and serve others. Jesus, I desire to partner with You in helping others follow You. I pray this in the name of the Father, and of the Son, and of the Holy Spirit. Amen.

INTRODUCTION – PART 2

by Dr. Tom Johnston

"Hear, O Israel: The LORD our God, the LORD is one. You shall love the LORD your God with all your heart and with all your soul and with all your might. And these words that I command you today shall be on your heart. You shall teach them diligently to your children, and shall talk of them when you sit in your house, and when you walk by the way, and when you lie down, and when you rise." (Deuteronomy 6:4-7)
As we begin to look at our "Rule of Life," The C.O.D.E., we need to understand the three elements which organize it:

1. *Affirmations from Scripture for daily reflection and prayer*
2. *Spiritual disciplines we will commit to embracing*
3. *Daily and weekly rhythms for engaging God in these disciplines*

The Affirmations are positive statements based on the Bible which indicate WHO we are as disciples of Christ and HOW we will pursue our life together with Him.

The Spiritual Disciplines are those things that we give ourselves to in pursuit of knowing and loving God, loving and serving others, and making disciples as part of our daily life. These are WHAT we will do in our pursuit of His way of life.

These are the two elements we will focus on in this devotional, the Affirmations and the Spiritual Disciplines giving us the WHO, the HOW, and the WHAT of the Jesus way of life.

The third element is the WHEN, the daily and weekly rhythms of the disciplines, and I want to focus on that in this second introductory section. Again, these patterns of spiritual pursuit are derived directly from the Scripture.

Daily Engagement

In developing our relationship with God, the practice of spiritual disciplines is essential. It is from this communion with God that we draw our strength to live life and engage in ministry. Our recommended pattern for daily personal and family spiritual disciplines is:

Reading the Scripture

Prayer, worship and quiet reflection in the Holy Spirit

Reading and reflecting on the affirmations found in The C.O.D.E.

Family reading and prayer with your spouse or children around meals, bedtimes, etc.

Weekly Engagement

As part of our way of life, our Community has gatherings weekly in the homes of members as well as other public places. Regular participation is how we make time and space for being with each other as we walk together in Christ. Many of the folks are together in aspects of everyday life or get together to study the Word or pray together. Our recommended pattern for weekly corporate spiritual disciplines is:

Regular participation in your church's worship celebration

Regular participation in a small group for discipleship

Participation in special life events of your church

The regular and consistent embrace of these spiritual rhythms will help you put down deep roots in the Lord, and empower you to live successfully as a disciple of Jesus. So, catch the rhythm.

Ask yourself these questions:

How am I doing with my spiritual rhythms? What do I need to change to embrace the Jesus way of life?

Pray this prayer:

Father God, thank you for teaching me Your way. Holy Spirit, guide me into making these spiritual practices part of my life every day and every week. Lord Jesus, help me organize my life around spending time with you! I pray this in the name of the Father, and of the Son, and of the Holy Spirit. Amen.

THE C.O.D.E

Christians Observing Disciplines Everyday

The Affirmations of a Disciple

Loving God (Matthew 22:34-40)

- "**I am a son/daughter of God**. I exist to love God with everything I am, and to be loved by Him with everything He is." (Matthew 6:9, John 1:12, 1 John 3:1a)
- "Before all things, I will seek first His Kingdom and righteousness, trusting Him for my needs." (Matthew 6:33)
- "I will seek to have my whole life become an act of worship." (Romans 12:1-2)
- "Knowing and loving God is my first priority."

Loving Others As You Love Yourself (Matthew 22:34-40)

- "**I am a servant.** I will love others with the love of Christ, seeking their welfare before my own." (Matthew 23:11, Philippians 2:1-11)
- "I will have a healthy appreciation of the self, based in my understanding of who I am in Christ." (1 John 3:1, Romans 12:3)

- "I will seek self-awareness through God-awareness." (1 Corinthians 13:12)
- "Loving and serving others is my second priority."

As You Go, Making Disciples (Matthew 28:18-20)

- **"I am a steward.** My mission as a disciple of Jesus Christ is to make more and better disciples for Him everywhere I go. It is the outworking of my loving devotion to Christ and His Church." (Matthew 28:18-20)
- "I will be a witness who shares with others the comfort that I myself have received from God through Jesus Christ." (Acts 1:8, 2 Corinthians 1:3-5, John 9:25)
- "Making disciples is my third priority."

In pursuit of this I will give myself to the practice of spiritual disciplines

1. "I submit my life to The Holy Scriptures - The Word of God."
2. "I will practice daily the presence of the Holy Spirit through reflective prayer."
3. "I will depend on the empowering presence of the Holy Spirit in my life and ministry."
4. "I am devoted to The Fellowship—living a shared life together in Christ as family and community."
5. "I am devoted to The Breaking of Bread—the celebration of the Lord's Supper and the practice of hospitality."
6. "I will practice generosity through tithing as a means

of personal discipline, giving offerings as an act of love and providing for the needs of others."

7. "I will lovingly, gently and graciously share with others the story of how God's love and grace has transformed my heart and life."

LOVING GOD

(Matthew 22:34-40)

"I am a son/daughter of God. I exist to love God with everything I am, and to be loved by Him with everything He is." (Matthew 6:9, John 1:12, 1 John 3:1a)

"Before all things, I will seek first His Kingdom and righteousness, trusting Him for my needs." (Matthew 6:33)

"I will seek to have my whole life become an act of worship." (Romans 12:1-2)

"Knowing and loving God is my first priority."

Loving God #1

by Dr. Tom Johnston

"I am a son/daughter of God. I exist to love God with everything I am, and to be loved by Him with everything He is."

Pray then like this: Our Father in heaven, hallowed be your name. (Matthew 6:9)

As someone who has been involved in Christian leadership for more than 40 years, I believe I have discovered the one key element for a healthy and productive life: understanding our personal identity in Christ. When we understand who we are in Christ, the beauty and fruitfulness of our life is truly astounding to behold. The keystone of our life is who we understand ourselves to be. This is the inner foundation of our function as a disciple of Jesus Christ: the knowledge of ourselves in Christ as revealed by the Holy Spirit. The life we live every day flows out of the self-knowledge provided by the Spirit. The Apostle Paul indicates that by God's grace expressed in Christ we have been adopted and have received the Holy Spirit:

For all who are led by the Spirit of God are sons of God. For you did not receive the spirit of slavery to fall back into fear, but you have received the Spirit of adoption as sons, by whom we cry, "Abba! Father!" The Spirit himself bears witness with our spirit that we are children of God, and if children, then heirs—heirs of God and fellow heirs with Christ, provided we suffer with him in order that we may also be glorified with him. (Romans 8:13-17)

It is to this grace that Paul appeals when challenged in his apostolic role, declaring, *"I am what I am by the grace of God."* (1 Corinthians 15:10a) He was convinced of who he was in Christ, and such realization empowered him. The "ontological knowing" of himself as an adopted son, as a co-heir with Christ, allowed him to face the hardships of his life and ministry – even opposition from Corinth, a church which the Lord established through him. Based on this, my "working definition" of identity is:

> *Identity: The core ontological reality derived as created beings, bearing the image of our Divine Father, and as His offspring, we are His children, His sons and daughters. ... The relationship with our Creator/Father is what ultimately defines us, giving us our core relational identity. (Johnston, Tom. The Way of the Master: The Leader Development Methodology of Jesus, p. 15. Kindle Edition.)*

So, how do we get there? How do we know ourselves in Christ? First, we have to understand that *we don't define ourselves; we discover who we are* – and that discovery comes to us by the revelation of God. Our attempts at self-definition are the greatest of sins. It stands to reason that we should press into the Lord, His Word, and the community of fellow disciples of Jesus around us. Thus, He may speak to us about who we are - not just in the general sense - but in the specific sense as individuals. For while there is significant commonality in our adoption in Christ, there is also a distinct identity for us individually, which Christ Himself reveals to us by all the aforementioned means, but also by the Holy Spirit as well. This is a foretaste, a "knowing in part" of the full knowledge that will come to us in the ultimate revelation of Christ:

> *'He who has an ear, let him hear what the Spirit says to the churches. To the one who conquers I will give some of the hidden manna, and I will give him a white stone, with a new name written on the stone that no one knows except the one who receives it.' (Revelation 2:17)*

Press in, dear Christ-follower, into the person of God that you might know Him more, and thereby come to know yourself more fully, becoming a healthy leader, secure in your identity, effective and fruitful in Him!

Ask yourself these questions:

How am I currently defining myself? Is it by what my Father says about me, or is it by other things?

Pray this prayer:

Most gracious Heavenly Father, thank You so much for including me in Your family. I ask that You reveal to me who You see me to be, through Your Word, Your Spirit, and Your people. Please expose those things by which I inappropriately define myself, and help me to discover who I am in You as Your child. Guide me into a greater understanding of who You have always intended me to be. I ask this in the name of the Father, and of the Son, and of the Holy Spirit. Amen.

Loving God #2

by Mike Chong Perkinson

"I am a son/daughter of God. I exist to love God with everything I am, and to be loved by Him with everything He is."

> *And when Jesus was baptized, immediately he went up from the water, and behold, the heavens were opened to him, and he saw the Spirit of God descending like a dove and coming to rest on him; and behold, a voice from heaven said, "This is my beloved Son, with whom I am well pleased." (Matthew 3:16-17)*

Have you ever been celebrated simply because you were a son or a daughter ... simply loved because you exist? You know, loved for no other reason than that you are someone's delight?

The baptism of Jesus lays out for us the basis of the Father's relationship with the Son and how Jesus, as the Son, lived His life in the love of the Father. The passage in Matthew 3 is profoundly beautiful as it declares the love that exists within the Godhead as the Spirit descends as a dove and the Father celebrates the Son.

All this, mind you, before Jesus had done anything official in ministry. Let me say it, shout it, the Father's love for the Son was not predicated upon His obedience. Nor is the Father's love for you. God's love for you cannot change. It simply is. God can be pleased and displeased with us, but never will His love change – NEVER!

Dare I say it? God celebrates you! Isn't that what He did on day 6 as He created Adam and Eve and stood back and declared how good, so very good, His masterpiece, His crowning work was. We are His masterpiece (Ephesians 2:10), works of art that were created from love to display the very love that fashioned us into existence.

Ask yourself these questions:

Who does the Father say that I am? What about me does God celebrate? What lies make that question difficult to answer? What fear, lie, pain, or wound keeps me from being able to experience the Father's love more fully?

Pray this prayer:

Father, I ask that You help me see myself the way You see me, forgiven and cleansed through the redeeming blood of Jesus. Help me to understand that my worth is not determined by what I do but by what You've done in and through Your Son. Help me to see that You celebrate me as Your masterpiece because You created me. Help me to confess and embrace my brokenness and surrender my sin and shame to You so that You might bring healing freedom and release to my life today. Amen.

Loving God #3

by Tim McGinnin Jr.

"I am a son/daughter of God. I exist to love God with everything I am, and to be loved by Him with everything He is."

But to all who did receive him, who believed in his name, he gave the right to become children of God... (John 1:12)

We are all children of God, sons and daughters of the King of kings and the Lord of lords. This is a foundational truth in Christianity, something we typically hear early in our walk with God and sometimes long before we have a relationship with the Lord. The statement "we are all God's children" can even sound cliché. But what does it mean to be a child of the living God?

In the above Scripture, we see that when we receive Him and believe in Him we get the right to become His children. We later learn, in another of the Apostle John's writings, that the identification of ourselves as children of God is a demonstration of the unconditional and matchless love that our Father in heaven has for us (1 John 3:1a). Being His child is not something that we can achieve for ourselves through anything that we do; but rather it is a gift that is given to us from God our Father.

To understand our identity as God's children, we must also understand who He is. God is the King and Creator of everything that exists (Psalm 47:2, 2 Timothy 6:15). God loves us so much, that He chose to give us the right to be His children; and if we are children of the King, then through this relationship we, as sons and daughters, are princes and princesses. We are children of the one true God and King of everything. Thus, to be loved by Him with everything He is, we have to accept the position that He has put us in as His children. We are meant to identify ourselves in this way first and foremost because it is how He sees us. When God looks at you, He immediately sees His child. We are

His sons and daughters. We are princes and princesses loved by our God, the King, more than anything else.

Ask yourself these questions:

How do I identify myself? When I first think of who I am, do I think about being God's child?

Pray this prayer:

Heavenly Father, thank You for choosing me to be Your child. Thank You for Your grace and for Your unconditional love. Help me to live my life in a way that I am always receiving Your love the way You have intended me to, and also to love You the way that You have intended me to. I claim the title of son/daughter that You have set apart for me. Help me to identify myself as Your son/daughter first and foremost, before any other title or role that I have. I ask this in the name of the Father, and of the Son, and of the Holy Spirit. Amen.

Loving God #4

by Selina McGinnin

"I am a son/daughter of God. I exist to love God with everything I am, and to be loved by Him with everything He is."

> *I will arise and go to my father, and I will say to him, "Father, I have sinned against heaven and before you. I am no longer worthy to be called your son. Treat me as one of your hired servants." And he arose and came to his father. But while he was still a long way off, his father saw him and felt compassion, and ran and embraced him and kissed him. And the son said to him, 'Father, I have sinned against heaven and before you. I am no longer worthy to be called your son.' But the father said to his servants 'Bring quickly the best robe, and put it on him, and put a ring on his hand, and shoes on his feet. And bring the fattened calf and kill it, and let us eat and celebrate. For this my son was dead, and is alive again; he was lost, and is found.' And they began to celebrate. (Luke 15:18-24)*

We can be pretty good at running, hiding and doing our own thing. We are a lot like the son in this parable at times. Sometimes we are so afraid to turn to God, our Father, for the first time or for a subsequent time. We feel shame, regret, or unworthy. We fear He will have had enough of us. We convince ourselves there is no coming back from what we've done. These are all lies. The story of the Prodigal Son reflects how our Father longs to be in relationship with us.

The Father saw the son and *RAN* towards his child and *EMBRACED* him. He didn't yell, condemn, or shame him. The Father welcomed him and immediately made him part of the family again. That right there is our Father's forgiveness, His mercy, and His grace. We are His. We are His sons and His daughters. There is nothing He wants more than for us to walk in relationship with Him as His children. We were made for it.

We come to the Father, admitting our need and our sin, just as the son in the story did, and the Father embraces us and gives us a place in His home and claim to an inheritance. We are well-loved children with a Father just waiting to run towards us as we come home to Him.

Ask yourself these questions:

What about the Father's reaction to the son stood out to me the most and why? How have I been hiding or running from God in ways that would keep me from a new or deeper relationship with Him?

Do I believe that God will receive me the same way the father in the story received his son? If it was hard to say "yes" to that question, why? What lie or prior hurt is keeping me from accepting His love for me?

Pray this prayer:

Father, thank You for love that continues to embrace me even when I think You must have had enough of me. Thank You for Your grace and mercy. Lord, help me to surrender to You and accept who You have called me to be and the place You have given me in Your Kingdom. Father I confess my sins to you. Forgive me, Lord. I choose to come home to You today. Clear the lies of the enemy from my thoughts and heal past hurts that would cause me to not embrace being Your son/daughter or accept You as a loving and forgiving Father. Amen.

Loving God #5

by Marjorie Clark

"I am a son/daughter of God. I exist to love God with everything I am, and to be loved by Him with everything He is."

> *See what kind of love the Father has given to us, that we should be called children of God; and so we are. (1 John 3:1a)*

The Apostle John is the apostle of love. Of all the disciples, he is the one who knew what it was to be loved by Jesus. He never left Jesus' side as He walked from the garden to the cross, to the last few minutes before His death when He said to His mother, "Woman, behold your son" and to "the disciple whom He loved," "Behold, your mother!" (John 19:26-27) Two days later he outraced Peter to the empty tomb, waited as Peter went in first, and then went in. He writes of himself, "and he saw and believed." (John 20:3-8)

The Father's love is a central theme in this epistle. He addresses us, his readers, as little children, dear children. That is the kind of love the Father has given to us – He says to you and to me, "come to Me, My dear child". We are first and foremost, in the Father's eyes, His dear children. His love for us is full of affection, devotion, delight. He wants us to come to Him, to be with Him at all times and receive His love. He has given us everything! And everything means He withholds nothing from us if we will receive His love. That is hard for us to understand. Even those of us who have had the best of parents might find it hard to approach this kind of love. There's nothing like it on earth. We put labels on it, we study it, we dramatize it, we re-define it, but rarely do we comprehend and embrace this kind of love.

I know but a few disciples of Jesus who have truly grasped the Father's love. It's transformational. The ones who have been transformed by it shine. You can see the difference between one who knows the Father's love and has been changed by it, and one who believes in and has studied and tried to be a good son or daughter but has yet to receive it. It saddens me, and it saddens our Father. He invites you, just come into His presence and be with Him. Be you with Him. Listen to Him. Talk with Him. I'm not talking about your prayer list. Our Father's love can only be received by being with Him.

I am a daughter of God and I exist to love Him with everything I am. In order to do that, I must receive His love as the child He delights in. He's not too busy for you. He's not ashamed of you. He's not disappointed in you. His love is so vastly different from our own. The only way to know it, and to love Him in return, is to begin living with Him as His child.

Ask yourself this question:

In what ways have I held back from being His child, and fully receiving and returning His love?

Pray this prayer:

Father, Your love for me is hard to imagine. I confess I have held back from being a child in Your presence. I've spent so much time trying to please You with my good behavior, my prayers, my studies. I've worked at loving You. Being a child in Your presence is a foreign concept to me. Yet, I am Your child. So, here I am. I'm coming to You as Your dear child. I'm ready to be loved by You with everything You are, so that I can love You, really love You, with everything I am. *(Keep the conversation going ...write down what You hear Him saying to you.)* ***Your love is amazing! Amen.***

Loving God #6

by Dr. Tom Johnston

"Before all things, I will seek first His Kingdom and righteousness, trusting Him for my needs."

> *"Therefore do not be anxious, saying, 'What shall we eat?' or 'What shall we drink?' or 'What shall we wear?' For the Gentiles seek after all these things, and your heavenly Father knows that you need them all. But seek first the kingdom of God and his righteousness, and all these things will be added to you." (Matthew 6:31-33)*

There is nothing more important than the Kingdom of God. This is a core truth of the Christian faith. Everything Jesus said and did was about seeing the Kingdom emerge in the Earth, and His instruction to us was that we were to make seeking the Kingdom a top priority. Rather than be consumed with the needs of daily life, making sure we had enough "stuff," He said we were to focus on God and His Kingdom.

When we focus on the things of God and living out the Kingdom way of life, the Father will meet our personal needs. We trust Him, rely upon Him, and understand that He is the source of all our provision. In fact, the term "righteousness" in this passage means to attend to the needs of others. So, as we focus on God and others, the Father makes sure we have everything we need for everyday life. This is yet another way that we demonstrate our love for Him: making His priorities our own, and organizing our life around what He values.

The Kingdom is so important that Jesus taught us to pray for it to come here on earth, where we are, right now today:

> *"Pray then like this: 'Our Father in heaven, hallowed be your name. Your kingdom come, your will be done, on earth as it is in heaven'." (Matthew 6:9-10)*

Prioritizing the Kingdom in our life, seeking after it, living out the Kingdom way of Jesus and, as part of that, caring for the needs of others is what the Father desires. It's how we love Him. So, remember this week that nothing is more important than the Kingdom of God. Seek it with everything you've got!

Ask yourself these questions:

Am I prioritizing seeking God and His Kingdom? What do I need to change in my life to be able to do so more fully? What do I need to let go of that is in the way?

Pray this prayer:

Father God, let Your Kingdom come, let Your will be done in my life. Use me to bring Your Kingdom to earth. Holy Spirit, make me aware of the needs of others around me so that I may live out Your love by caring for them. I trust You for my needs. Please forgive me for placing other things before You and Your Kingdom. I ask that You change my heart so that You and Your Kingdom are first in my life. I pray this in the name of the Father, and of the Son, and of the Holy Spirit. Amen.

Loving God #7

by Tim McGinnin Jr.

"Before all things, I will seek first His Kingdom and righteousness, trusting Him for my needs."

Therefore I tell you, do not be anxious about your life, what you will eat or what you will drink, nor about your body, what you will put on...But seek first the kingdom of God and his righteousness, and all these things will be added to you. (Matthew 6: 25, 33)

Have you ever been worried about paying your bills, putting gas in your car, or buying food and clothes? Many of us deal with this type of worry at one point or another in our lives. It's not that we enjoy worrying. For the most part, we would usually say that we can't help it. We get so consumed in the day-to-day grind of life that we end up putting quite a bit of pressure on ourselves to make it all work. But what if it wasn't your job to make it work? What if God owned the responsibility of taking care of us, and we only needed to be obedient to His will in the moment and allow Him to take care of us? That's exactly what Jesus says.

Read Matthew 6:25-34 in its entirety and you will see Jesus paint a picture for us of a loving Father who created and provided for everything in all of creation from the birds of the air to the flowers and the grass on the ground. None of these things bear the image that we do—the Image of God (Genesis 1:27). It is this very image that the Father cherishes in us as His children so deeply, beyond anything else. If God is going to take care of all of these other elements of creation, how could He not take care of that which He loves and cares for the most?

Something that is easy to miss in this section of Scripture is the fact that all of these things that God takes care of—the animals and the plants—are all being taken care of within the context and purpose for which they were created. The same is true for us. It is when we are aligned with our loving Father's will for our lives, when we are obedient to seeking first His Kingdom, that we are in the center of His care and provision. Thus, when we are following Jesus in the way that He set before us, there is no need to be anxious about food or clothing, or the mortgage, or anything else! When we put the Kingdom of God first, all of our needs will be met by our loving Father. "The Lord is good to all, and his mercy is over all that he has made." (Psalm 145:9)

Ask yourself these questions:

What are the things in my life that I'm worrying about right now? What would it look like for me to walk in obedience to God's will for my life right now?

Pray this prayer:

Heavenly Father, thank You for loving me and caring for me as Your child. Thank you for meeting all of my needs out of Your love. Lord, help me to not worry about the things that I need from day to day, but rather help me focus on Your Kingdom and Your will for my life. Show me what it looks like to seek Your Kingdom first on a daily basis and help me to trust You deeply and without wavering. I ask this in the name of the Father, and of the Son, and of the Holy Spirit. Amen.

Loving God #8

by John Kimball

"Before all things, I will seek first His Kingdom and righteousness, trusting Him for my needs."

Do not be anxious about anything, but in everything by prayer and supplication with thanksgiving let your requests be made known to God. And the peace of God, which surpasses all understanding, will guard your hearts and your minds in Christ Jesus. (Philippians 4:6-7)

There were days and nights when this verse was all I had to hang onto. I questioned everything in my life: my decisions, my calling, my sanity... But the Holy Spirit guarded the depths of my faith. God's Word, at least certain portions of it, broke through the din in my head and ministered to me. This went on for nearly two years.

Clinical anxiety is a horrible thing. I've learned a lot about it over the last few years. It can be caused by trauma, tragedy, brain chemistry – and, I believe, spiritual attack. Such anxiety can find a spot to anchor – in any place where one has stopped trusting God. My family has a history of anxiety over four generations. It was time for this curse to be broken.

There is so much more to my story, but the bottom line is that I had to identify where the root was in my own life. And this required me to venture into areas I preferred to avoid. You see, anxiety – even if it is physiologically caused – feeds and grows on a lack of trust. I used medication, and it helped. I saw more than one counselor, and they gave me critical guidance. But it was when I turned many different (important) areas of my life over to my Heavenly Father and chose to trust Him that I began to emerge from anxiety's mire.

Philippians 4:6-7 are great verses. But it's easier recited than put into practice – especially if you are currently suffering. The words, “Don’t be anxious about anything…” are all-encompassing. And Paul means what he says, because Jesus taught it to him (Matthew 6:25-34). Trusting in everything is not easy. It’s not natural. It’s a decision we make in faith. We learn to pray differently. We learn to give thanks in all circumstances. And when we do, we learn that our Heavenly Father is trust*worthy*. He’ll prove it again and again. Then, slowly and beautifully, we begin to experience real peace as the Father guards our hearts and our minds in Jesus.

Ask yourself these questions:

Am I anxious? Is it extreme? What are the things in my life that trigger it the most? What steps am I taking to mitigate its symptoms? And more importantly, what steps am I taking to learn to fully and completely trust God to take care of my triggers?

Pray this prayer:

Abba Father, my anxiety tells me, among other things, that I am not trusting You. My mind is consumed with “what ifs” and fear. Help me to see what I’m struggling to do on my own. Draw me close and give me peace. Enable me to identify all those concerns I need to give to You in prayer, and then to turn them over to You. Thank You for guarding my heart and my mind in Christ Jesus. Amen.

Loving God #9

by Dr. Tom Johnston

"Before all things, I will seek first His Kingdom and righteousness, trusting Him for my needs."

Kingdoms have a king, which seems to be logical, right? Sometimes it is tough for us to get our head around what that actually looks like. Kings and queens in the Western world today are primarily figureheads, albeit important ones, from a former age. As such, they don't have any real power; they don't call the shots. Unlike the days of old, most monarchs today have little or no impact on the day-to-day life of people. In the United States, it's been about 250 years since we kicked George III back to England. Today, if we don't like a President, we just vote them out of office. So, when we say "Jesus is my King," we may not really understand how much of a wide-reaching impact that has on our lives.

First of all, *kings get to tell you what to do*; they set the priorities of their subjects. A king defines what is important to them, and the focus of those in their Kingdom revolves around that. Now, if you serve a good king, their priorities focus on establishing their reign and rule for the benefit of their subjects. If you are subject to a bad king, well, then from a historical perspective, it's usually all about them. Jesus is the Good King and has established His Kingdom because of love. He was motivated by love for His Father, looking to re-establish His dominion on Earth. And also love for humanity, working on setting us free from the oppressive rule of the Enemy:

> *And so, from the day we heard, we have not ceased to pray for you, asking that you may be filled with the knowledge of his will in all spiritual wisdom and understanding, so as to walk in a manner worthy of the Lord, fully pleasing to him: bearing fruit in every good work and increas-*

ing in the knowledge of God; being strengthened with all power, according to his glorious might, for all endurance and patience with joy; giving thanks to the Father, who has qualified you to share in the inheritance of the saints in light. He has delivered us from the domain of darkness and transferred us to the kingdom of his beloved Son, in whom we have redemption, the forgiveness of sins. (Colossians 1:9-14)

We reciprocate the love of our Good King Jesus by responding to Him and His expectations for us as His subjects. Jesus said: *"If you love me, you will keep my commandments".* (John 14:15) We allow Him to prioritize our lives, aligning us with His will. And we passionately seek His dominion – because of our love for Him – but also because as we surrender more of our heart, our minds, and our lives to His authority, we gain more degrees of freedom from the Kingdom of Darkness.

So, the Kingdom has a King, and He is good and has the right to rule over His creation – *which means us.* As we make His Kingdom our priority, this Good King will attend to everything we need. He will care for the practical things of life and be our defense against the Enemy of our soul. So, seek first the Kingdom – because the King is good!

Ask yourself these questions:

Do I really think Jesus is a good King? Do I trust Him to rule over me completely?

Pray this prayer:

Father God, let Your Kingdom come, let Your will be done in my life. I acknowledge that You are a good King and that it is in Your Kingdom that I find safety and provision. Holy Spirit, I ask that You lead me to continually submit myself to Christ's dominion. I pray this in the name of the Father, and of the Son, and of the Holy

Spirit. Amen.

Loving God #10

by Selina McGinnin

"Before all things, I will seek first His Kingdom and righteousness, trusting Him for my needs."

"Do not lay up for yourselves treasures on earth, where moth and rust destroy and where thieves break in and steal, but lay up for yourselves treasures in heaven, where neither moth nor rust destroys and where thieves do not break in and steal. For where your treasure is, there your heart will be also. (Matthew 6:19-21)

Life can be so distracting, can't it? We want to explore, have success, have new things, achieve our dreams, find love, start families, and the list goes on. We split our focus and our time among so many things. We get so tired, so discontent, so full of anxiety trying to accomplish the things we have set out to do. We place our treasures, or priorities, on the things that will fade and not on what will last forever. We all get distracted here and lose focus. Jesus wouldn't have covered it in His teachings if struggling with the above wasn't going to be an obstacle for us.

We must be a resolved people who prioritize our lives according to the Kingdom of God. We must choose daily to prioritize God's plan over our own. There is a phrase I have adopted whenever I start to struggle between doing what I want and what I know God is calling to me – "Only you, Lord." In this simple phrase, I refocus myself first by recognizing God's lordship over my life. If He is Lord, why am I questioning Him? If I believe He is good, why am I trying to convince myself that my plan is better? Second, I remind myself that only He is my focus, He is my treasure. When He is my focus, my family is better served, my friends and my community are better served, and I am less stressed out because in Him I have found my contentment. *Only you, Lord.*

Too many of us often put our time and energy into things that, in the end, don't matter in the least. I recently spoke with someone, who is facing very aggressive Stage 4 cancer and one of the things she said to me was "I feel like I've wasted so much of my life. All that I care about now is people knowing about Jesus and doing what He has called me to do."

That's the laser focus and devotion to the Kingdom of God we need to strive for. Aim for the restoration of people to their Father and right relationship with one another. As we go, God will provide for us exactly what we need and for the needs of others.

Ask yourself these questions:

What do my current priorities look like? Does it align with where God is calling me? How is God asking me to refocus on Him and His purposes and say "Only You, Lord?" How can I serve God in my marriage, my parenting, my friendships, my workplace, my school, my hobbies?

Pray this prayer:

Father, I'm sorry for the things that I have placed before You. Show me how to re-prioritize my life so that it aligns with Your will and Your Kingdom. Lord, I don't want to waste my life but want to share Your Truth everywhere I go. Lord, help me to trust Your plan and trust that it is better than mine. You are a good God to supply my every need. Thank You, Lord. Amen.

Loving God #11

by Dr. Tom Johnston

"I will seek to have my whole life become an act of worship."

Most of the time when we think of the word "worship" what comes to mind is the music and singing which is such a vital part of when we gather together with other disciples of Jesus. Indeed, this wonderful action of love is what I would call expressive worship. Any time we gather with other disciples, and even when we are alone with the Lord, this is good and appropriate for us to do. We love Him, and it's okay to tell Him!

However, our worship isn't limited to these times, or to singing and praising Him. What God is actually looking for is that we would live our lives as worship. Everything we think, everything we do should be God-honoring, and as such, becomes worship. Jesus said two really big things about this. The first is in a conversation with the woman Samaria at the well of Jacob. She got really religious with Him, asking about the proper way of ritual worship. He told her this:

> *"But the hour is coming, and is now here, when the true worshipers will worship the Father in spirit and truth, for the Father is seeking such people to worship him. God is spirit, and those who worship him must worship in spirit and truth" (John 4:23-24).*

When Jesus said to her "in spirit and in truth" what He was saying was that the rituals didn't matter. Real worship *comes from the heart* (spirit) and takes the form of *real actions (truth).* We live our whole life from a loving heart of gratitude for who God is and what He has done for us. This is in line with what Jesus told us in the First Great Commandment. Here is what He said in responding to an expert in the Law of Moses:

> *And he said to him, "You shall love the Lord your God with all your heart and with all your soul and with all your mind. This is the great and first commandment" (Matthew 22:37-39).*

We love God with everything we are – our whole life – because He has already loved us with everything He is in Jesus Christ. We cannot have any "idols" in our lives – things that we worship other than God Himself. All of our time, talent, treasure, our inner thought life, our relationships, our jobs – everything – is to be an expression of our love for Him. This is true worship.

Ask yourself these questions:

Are there parts of my life which are not aligned with God's heart? How do I worship in my way of life, my thoughts, my intentions? What things other than God do I give my life to?

Pray this prayer:

Father God, let my whole life become an expression of my love for You. May what I think and how I live be pleasing to You. May my thoughts and actions align with Your will. Forgive me for my idolatry. Holy Spirit, please show me where I am worshipping something other than the Father. I pray this in the name of the Father, and of the Son, and of the Holy Spirit. Amen.

Loving God #12

by Tim McGinnin Jr.

"I will seek to have my whole life become an act of worship."

> *I appeal to you therefore, brothers, by the mercies of God, to present your bodies as a living sacrifice, holy and acceptable to God, which is your spiritual worship. (Romans 12:1)*

As Christians, we often think of worship as a genre of music or the act of singing a series of songs to God on a Sunday morning right before the pastor preaches a sermon; something to ramp us up before hearing the Bible taught to us. The reality though, is that singing to God is only a small part of what worship is actually meant to be. More specifically, it is one way that we express our worship to a living and loving God. Worship is much bigger than singing though. It is much more holistic—it is meant to be the entirety of how we live our lives.

In the Old Testament, we read of a time when animal sacrifices were to be used as a means of atonement for our sins. There were specific animals to be used for particular occasions, and these animals had to be a certain way (i.e. a lamb without blemish). The right type of animal at the right time was considered a holy and acceptable offering to God as it was given up on the altar. In Romans, Paul is telling us that we are to present our own selves in a certain and particular way to God. We are to be "a living sacrifice." This means that we don't have to physically die—Jesus already did that for us—but it also means that we have to give ourselves up to God in a different way. *We have to give God every aspect of our being.* This means that we live in such a way that everything we are and in everything that we do, we are seeking to honor God: with *every action, every thought, and every breath.* This is how we become holy and acceptable to the Lord in the way that we live.

It is in this very act, or rather series of acts and choices in our daily lives, that we are engaged in this spiritual worship, this giving of our whole selves over to God. This process is a major part of our journey as Christians that we won't fully realize until we are with the Lord in eternity. Our job however, in the here and now, is to identify *where in our lives we are worshipping God and where we need to bring ourselves in worship to God.* We can see that worship really is so much more than singing a few songs —it is giving our whole selves over to Jesus and committing all of our thoughts and actions, our whole selves to His Kingdom purposes.

Ask yourself this question:

What areas of my life do I need to give over to God to worship Him more fully?

Pray this prayer:

Gracious Father, thank You for Your mercy and love in giving Jesus on the cross so that I would not have to die for my sins. Help me to bring myself into closer relationship with You so that I can present myself as holy and acceptable to You. Lord, I want to be a living sacrifice. I devote myself to You above all else and ask You to show me how to fully live my life to You—help me to worship You with my whole being. In the name of the Father, and of the Son, and of the Holy Spirit. Amen.

Loving God #13

by Marjorie Clark

"I will seek to have my whole life become an act of worship."

> *Therefore be imitators of God, as beloved children. And walk in love, as Christ loved us and gave himself up for us, a fragrant offering and sacrifice to God. (Ephesians 5:1-2)*

When reading scripture, I learned long ago to ask, "What is the "therefore" there for?" In this particular verse, "therefore" refers to Paul's previous exhortation to put away, or put behind us, our sinful and foolish behavior and speech, and instead to be kind and tenderhearted and forgiving – remembering that we are forgiven. How do we do this successfully? And why?

Why? Because our lives matter. How we live our lives matters. We are God's beloved children. Hear that? His *beloved children!* As such, our heart's desire is to be just like Him. Children naturally learn to be like their parents. They do that by observing their parents' posture, facial expressions, voices, responses and reactions, conversations, and behaviors. Without realizing it, children also 'log' their own emotional responses to their parents. All of this is recorded in their brains ... and eventually it is imitated in their own play, behavior, and relationships. Sometimes to the chagrin of their parents, children are the great imitators!

Our Father is love. He is good. He showed us His love in His Son, Christ Jesus, who gave His life for us. The sacrifice of Jesus was a fragrant offering and sacrifice to God which resulted in our becoming His beloved children. *Therefore,* as we imitate God, we walk in the love with which Christ loved us. We walk in that love toward our Father. We walk in that love toward others. *A sacrificial love.* As we do, our lives, like Christ's, become a sweet-smelling offering of sacrificial worship to God. It's a *whole-life act of walking in love*, in our thoughts, our speech, our choices, our responses, our relationships; in the moments when no one is watching and the moments when everyone is watching; in the moments when we are hurting and in the moments when we are celebrating; in our lack and in our abundance; in our moments of doubt and in our moments of faith; in our moments of anger and in our moments of forgiveness; in moments of birth and in moments of death ... *our lives are a love offering to God who has called us His beloved children.*

Ask yourself this question:

What is one area of my life where I am not imitating my Father God, and how can I walk in love in that area?

Pray this prayer:

Loving Father, thank You for saying I am Your beloved child. I want every part of my life to be pleasing to You. I know that I am struggling with walking in love in ________________. Please show me what is happening and why. I ask You to forgive me for not imitating Your love in this area. Thank You for Your forgiveness. Teach me, Holy Spirit. Direct my thoughts to Your thoughts and ways. Thank You for hearing me and loving me so completely. I ask that my whole life would be a pleasing sacrifice of worship to You in the name of Jesus, I pray. Amen.

Loving God #14

by Troy Sonnleitner

"I will seek to have my whole life become an act of worship."

I appeal to you therefore, brothers, by the mercies of God, to present your bodies as a living sacrifice, holy and acceptable to God, which is your spiritual worship. Do not be conformed to this world, but be transformed by the renewal of your mind, that by testing you may discern what is the will of God, what is good and acceptable and perfect. (Romans 12:1-2)

Humble yourselves before the Lord, and he will exalt you. (James 4:10)

I came out of a Roman Catholic background, which means that my frame of reference for religion was based on outward religious practice done in public. I don't believe outward religious practice is all bad if informed by our faith and love of Jesus. I departed the Roman Catholic church in my late teens. After several years of partying and pushing the boundaries of right and wrong, I had a jailhouse conversion. I devoted myself to Christ and I carried this outward/performance mindset with me into my newfound Protestant/Pentecostal church community. I had a drive to draw closer to Jesus but my impression was that in order to do so, I needed to be in the church building as often as it was open; like a "Good Catholic Boy" would. With a whole whopping six months under my belt of following Jesus I had a conversation with my dad. I gave him the "penance" list of how I had turned myself around. I was, of course, trying to justify myself with the public religious practice, assuming he would be affirming and maybe even impressed.

After listening, he said, "I'm glad you are expressing faith in Jesus and filling your time with good things instead of what you were before. I do think what's more important in my opinion, and probably God's, is *what you do when your 'feet hit the floor'.*" He then described his own epiphany of faith, and which he determined to put into practice every day as he put his feet on the floor after waking up. He would devote the day to Jesus and assert that it was His (God's) and that He sought what God's will was for the day. I was immediately challenged to remember this faith I now had was a personal relationship with Jesus first. As my dad often did, he blew me away with his simple wisdom.

My dad was not a what some would call a "religious" man but He loved Jesus and used whatever influence he had to point people to Christ. His knowledge of "the Good Book" and his character made the most skeptical people want to know what fueled his faith. I'm constantly reminded of this ideal of "Feet Hit the Floor". Often, I do well in devoting each day to Jesus, sometimes not so much. But whether the day starts out well or I'm reminded part way through, I still hear my dad's encouraging voice, "What's important is that you devote your day to Jesus 'when your feet hit the floor'."

Ask yourself these questions:

Am I devoting my day to Jesus? Am I submitting myself under His Lordship when my feet hit the floor?

Pray this prayer:

Lord Jesus, today, and every day is Yours, You are the Lord of my life. This is my act of worship and I thank You for giving me the Holy Spirit to remind me and guide me toward this ideal and gesture every morning. Amen!

Loving God #15

by Dr. Tom Johnston

"I will seek to have my whole life become an act of worship."

Sometimes the idea of "worship" is hard to get our head around. In the New Testament, the word worship means that we posture ourselves in body, attitude, and allegiance towards God. Such worship is an expression of our loving devotion to Him. In body, mind, and spirit, we bow before our King.

What we do with our body, all the actions of our life, we do out of love for Him:

> *...for you were bought with a price. So glorify God in your body. (1 Corinthians 6:20)*

The thoughts which fill our mind should reflect our passion for Him:

> *Finally, brothers, whatever is true, whatever is honorable, whatever is just, whatever is pure, whatever is lovely, whatever is commendable, if there is any excellence, if there is anything worthy of praise, think about these things. (Philippians 4:8)*

The passion and desires of our hearts should not be caught up in this world, but be for the things of God:

> *For all that is in the world—the desires of the flesh and the desires of the eyes and pride of life—is not from the Father but is from the world. And the world is passing away along with its desires, but whoever does the will of God abides forever. (1 John 2:16-17)*

The totality of who we are in body, mind, and spirit should align with Him and His will; this expresses our loving devotion to Him. The decisions we make on what we do with our body, the thoughts that we allow to fill our minds, and the things we desire in our hearts are influenced by our love for God. And all of these things are how we worship Him. This is what true worship really is, and all because of how much He has loved us in Christ! Set your body, mind, and spirit to worship him today!

Ask yourself these questions:

How do I worship God in my body, mind, and spirit? What are the things I do, what are the thoughts that I think, and what are the passions in my heart which do not honor God?

Pray this prayer:

Father God, let my whole life become an expression of my love for You. May what I do with my body, what I think with my mind, and what I desire in my heart honor You. Holy Spirit, align what I do, think, and feel with my Father's will. I pray this in the name of the Father, and of the Son, and of the Holy Spirit. Amen.

Loving God #16

by Dr. Tom Johnston

"Knowing and loving God is my first priority."

The whole reality of life is organized around our Creator. Everything is from Him and everything is for Him. As created beings we don't define ourselves nor should we organize our lives around our own passions and desires. It is the priorities which the Lord has for us that serve as the framework for how we live each day.

Knowing God is first and foremost the most important of all our priorities. In knowing Him we come to know ourselves, discover our purpose, and live out the existence for which we were created. We can only know God if He reveals Himself to us:

> *All things have been handed over to me by my Father, and no one knows the Son except the Father, and no one knows the Father except the Son and anyone to whom the Son chooses to reveal him. (Matthew 11:27)*

He reveals Himself in a general sense through creation, yet people still reject Him (Romans 1:20-21). He has revealed Himself most fully through the Son (Philippians 2:5-11), and the Son has given us the Holy Spirit who will lead us into all truth about God (John 16:12-15). The Spirit has given us the Scripture to guide us in the way of life to which Jesus has called us (2 Timothy 3:16-17). And the same Holy Spirit lives in and speaks through His community, the Church, as we live and learn in community (Ephesians 1:23). Coming to know God through the Spirit, the Word and the Church is essential. We must prioritize our day so as to make room for encounter with the Holy Spirit through the practice of spiritual disciplines and spending time with other disciples of Jesus. This is our first priority in our day.

As we grow in our knowledge of God and His love for us, we grow in our knowledge of Him. We love because He first loved us (1 John 4:19), and out of a heart of genuine thankfulness, we love God in return. It follows then that loving Him is a priority, and *love for Him prioritizes our life*. Thought, intention, action, and behavior all flow from a heart of grateful love. When we organize how we live around Him and His way, we demonstrate our love for Him, as Jesus said *"If you love me, you will keep my commandments"* (John 14:15). Simple obedience to Christ is how we love Him.

So, prioritize knowing God today so that you might love Him more and more. Let knowing and loving Him organize your day, your week, your year – your life. Make Him first – and watch everything else fall into place!

Ask yourself these questions:

What do I need to do to know God better? How am I doing in seeking to know and love Him more?

Pray this prayer:

Father God, please reveal Yourself to me that I might get to know You more. Reveal yourself through Your Spirit, Your Word and Your people, the Church. Help me understand the love which You have for me, that I might love You in return. I pray this in the name of the Father, and of the Son, and of the Holy Spirit. Amen.

Loving God #17

by Dr. Tom Johnston

"Knowing and loving God is my first priority."

There is a significant difference between knowing about someone, and truly knowing them. One is information, but the other is so much more – it requires relationship. As we seek to know God, we must learn about Him, but then we must move into an encounter with Him. It was for this that we were made – to live in relationship with the Creator. Because of this our relationship with God becomes the primary "organizing principle" of our lives.

We pursue *knowing about* Him through reading and studying His Word, the Bible:

> *Your word is a lamp to my feet and a light to my path. (Psalm 119:105)*

There has to be a significant, regular and consistent amount of time invested in learning about who He is. It can take many formats – *personal Bible reading and study, small group studies, sermons from your pastor* – but it will require dedicated time.

As we read the Word, we can press into the next aspect – *building our relationship* with Him. Like all relationships, if you want to get to know someone at a personal level, you have to spend time with them. The same is true with God – and we do this through prayer. Prayer is that ongoing conversation with Him, a dialog of speaking and listening, and we need to prioritize time with Him:

> *The eyes of the LORD are toward the righteous and his ears toward their cry. (Psalm 34:15)*

He is always ready to engage in the conversation, and always available to be with you in prayer. As the Holy Spirit resides within each disciple of Jesus, prayer can happen in any place at any time. However, establishing regular patterns of prayer is a matter of spiritual discipline.

Building our relationship with God takes time and energy, and must become our first priority. We must organize our daily and weekly life around it. As we learn about Him, and know Him personally, we grow in our love for Him!

Ask yourself these questions:

Are the Word and prayer actual priorities for me? How am I doing in prioritizing my time to know Him more?

Pray this prayer:

Father God, thank You for the wonderful gift of Your Scriptures, that I might learn about You. Holy Spirit thank you for making prayer possible. Teach me to set daily practices for being in the Word and in prayer, that I might grow in my relationship with You. I pray this in the name of the Father, and of the Son, and of the Holy Spirit. Amen.

Loving God #18

by Tim McGinnin Jr.

"Knowing and loving God is my first priority."

You shall love the Lord your God with all your heart and with all your soul and with all your might. (Deuteronomy 6:5)

What is the most important thing you must accomplish today? If you are anything like me, that question creates a barrage of tasks and projects that are on your list of things to get done. Some of the items on your list are new; maybe you just added them today. Others have been lingering and compiling for what seems like forever. There never seems to be enough time to get everything done on the list, right? It's simply ever-growing and there are always things competing for our time and attention. Our lists represent things of value to us. We spend the time on the things that are important. And if something is among the highest priorities that you have, it gets tackled first, or at least sooner. In reflecting on your priorities for the day, where does spending time with the Lord fall on your list? Does He even make the list? Does your relationship with the Lord represent the first priority in your life?

We hear the command to love the Lord from Deuteronomy echoed by Jesus in the Gospel of Matthew in what we know as the first part of The Great Commandments. This was so familiar, so well-known and understood by the hearer of His day. It was nothing new and it wasn't surprising. Jesus said that loving God was "the great and first commandment" (Matthew 22:28). It is of higher import than any other thing on the list of priorities in life. This would have resonated deeply for the Jewish hearer of the day. It was something they had been taught as early as they could remember, and they would have recited it daily as part of their rhythms of prayer and worship. It was ingrained in their lives. For followers of Jesus today, this should not be a foreign concept. *Of course we are to love God first*! It is what we have been taught since the beginning of our walk with Jesus, whenever that may have begun. It is among the most fundamental truths that we believe and the command of Scripture is clear — we are to love the Lord with everything that we are and everything that we have. *But how does that play out as a priority in your life?* Do the things you focus on throughout your day demonstrate loving the Lord with every aspect of your being? Can you point to the things you accomplished yesterday and confidently say "Yesterday, knowing and loving God was my first priority based on the way that I lived my life"? Will you be able to say that about today? If loving the Lord our God with everything that we are is indeed our first priority, we will be able to say, "this is how I lived that out."

Ask yourself these questions:

What are the things in my life that get prioritized before my relationship with the Lord? How can I align my life better to keep the Lord as my first priority?

Pray this prayer:

Lord, forgive me for putting anything else above and before You in my life. Thank You for Your gracious love and mercy and for calling me Your child. Help me to properly value the love that You give me by loving You and choosing You first in every aspect of my life. Holy Spirit, transform my heart and renew my mind, so that I might keep You first for all of my days. I pray this in the name of the Father, and of the Son, and of the Holy Spirit. Amen.

Loving God #19

by Selina McGinnin

"Knowing and loving God is my first priority."

Depending on the season of life, our priorities shift. We are always adjusting to what we are currently walking through. Schooling, children, work deadlines or advancement, home buying or repairing, family needs, personal care, pets, the list goes on as to what demands our time and attention and how soon. The list never really stays the same for too long or in the same order. Emergencies pop up, unexpected circumstances arise and we must shift to accommodate. This can be stressful and sometimes these variables take us out emotionally or mentally. Often, we feel the stress and tension greater than we ought because we have our priorities in the wrong order.

Augustine's writings on *rightly ordered love* can be directly applied to the above. The right ordering of love is the idea that we place what ought to be loved in a rightful place, not too excessive, not too deficient, and not misdirected, but instead rightly ordered. *The correct order in any set of loves is to have God placed in the number one spot. God in any other spot would be disordered love.*

When we place God as our first love and as our first priority, it alters our behaviors. Our behaviors are directly linked to our heart and our heart motivates the direction of our lives and the choices we make. By placing God first, we learn to love and enjoy what God has made and given us. It becomes less about what we do and don't have, or have and haven't achieved, and more about what we have been given and who the Giver is. The change in both our behaviors and hearts through *rightly ordering our loves in turn eases the tensions we feel created by trying to balance the challenges and duties of this life.* This shift in thinking aids us to live in the tension of the in-between of the now and the eternal. What is now will fade, it will not last. Our focus must be on the eternal and the One who never changes and will never fade. Our true Treasure.

> *"Do not lay up for yourselves treasures on earth, where moth and rust destroy and where thieves break in and steal, but lay up for yourselves treasures in heaven, where neither moth nor rust destroys and where thieves do not break in and steal. For where your treasure is there your heart will be also." (Matthew 6:19-21)*

We must never forget that God is ultimately the one who changes hearts. It is only in our pursuit of Him that we will recognize this shift in our lives. As Augustine says in *Confessions, X.29:*

> *"O Love ever burning, never quenched! O Charity, my God, set me on fire with your love! You command me to be content. Give me the grace to do as you command, and command me to do what you will!"*

Ask yourself these questions:

Where do I spend most of my time and energy? Is God currently my first love? If not what/who is being placed before Him?

Pray this prayer:

Father, forgive me for placing anything before You. Come and fill me with Your love, may I know it and feel it in a new and refreshing way. Create in me a heart that pursues You first and places You above all others and all other ambitions. I lay my heart at Your feet. I surrender to You, Lord. Amen.

Loving God #20

by Marjorie Clark

"Knowing and loving God is my first priority."

But seek first the kingdom of God and his righteousness, and all these things will be added to you. (Matthew 6:33)

We love because he first loved us. (1 John 4:19)

Priorities. We seldom think about them directly, but they are a compelling part of every decision we make, whether it concerns money, relationships, time, careers, where we live or where we worship. Jesus addressed priorities often and we see His teaching in this definitive statement concerning priorities. "Seek first the kingdom of God and his righteousness ..." This Scripture is often associated with our 'devotions'. Yet, Jesus doesn't mention worship or reading the Word of God in this discourse. A closer look reveals that He is talking about the 'necessities' of life, food and clothing. Oh, and right in the middle of it He mentions the "span of life" – how long you live – saying you cannot add even an hour to it. He is not known for His subtlety, but He is known for taking things a step further than expected.

Why? Because He loves us. He loved us first, before we even knew His name. And His love compels Him to care for us, to provide for us, and to give us understanding about the kingdom of God so that we can get our priorities straight. When I seek first the kingdom of God and His righteousness, I'll make the right decisions about my daily rhythms, because I know His love and I love Him and want to put Him first. Whether it's the first few minutes of the day or that hour in the middle of the day, or that evening time after the children are in bed and the house is quiet – my heart will be directed to Him and we will spend the best part of the day together.

When we experience His love and we know Him intimately, we always give Him the best part of ourselves and our time and our resources. We don't give it away to anything or anyone else. It is holy unto Him. It's not a matter of checking off the boxes – devotions X, church X, tithe X, prayers X – and then going on our way. No? No. Seeking first His kingdom and His righteousness is 24/7/365 living because knowing Him and loving Him is our life and breath and our great priority at all times. Yes?

Ask yourself this question:

In what areas of my 24/7/365 life is knowing and loving God NOT my first priority?

Pray this prayer:

God Almighty, my Creator, my Redeemer, my Provider, I confess that I don't even know how to begin to seek You and Your kingdom first in every area of my life. I humble myself before You and ask Your forgiveness for my unbelief and my self-centered life. Thank You for loving me first, and for love that is steadfast – never giving up on me! What now, Lord? What do I need to do next to truly seek You first? I'm listening so that I might obey. You alone are worthy, O Lord! Amen.

LOVING OTHERS AS YOU LOVE YOURSELF

(Matthew 22:34-40)

"I am a servant. I will love others with the love of Christ, seeking their welfare before my own." *(Matthew 23:11, Philippians 2:1-11)*

"I will have a healthy appreciation of the self, based in my understanding of who I am in Christ." *(1 John 3:1, Romans 12:3)*

"I will seek self-awareness through God-awareness." *(1 Corinthians 13:12)*

"Loving and serving others is my second priority."

Loving Others As You Love Yourself #1

by Dr. Tom Johnston

"I am a servant. I will love others with the love of Christ, seeking their welfare before my own."

The culture of the Kingdom of God is so vastly different from the culture of this world. The difference is truly amazing, and can be seen quite clearly in this statement which Jesus makes to His disciples: "The greatest among you shall be your servant." (Matthew 23:11) Hearing this was shocking for a bunch of guys who were jockeying for position in the new political order they thought Jesus was about to establish. As a group, they were functioning in the "me-first," self-absorbed agenda of the rest of fallen humanity. They didn't get it – they didn't understand the self-sacrificing, other-oriented character of Kingdom life.

In everything He did, Jesus put us before Himself. He became human, which was to embrace an eternal self-limitation. He put up with a bunch of whiny guys who just didn't have a clue about what He was up to, all while He focused on the healing, deliverance, and salvation of other people. The only person He was more jealous for than humanity was His Father, and He did what He did for us because of the Father's love for us (ref. John 3:16). In everything, Jesus set the model for His disciples to be servants of one another; not to be masters, or lords, or some other exalted title, but to serve one another. By this they would continually demonstrate His love, and thereby people would know that they were His disciples:

> *A new commandment I give to you, that you love one another: just as I have loved you, you also are to love one another. By this all people will know that you are my disciples, if you have love for one another." (John 13:34-35)*

When we serve others, we demonstrate the servant heart of Jesus, and best exemplify God's loving, compassionate, self-sacrificing nature. If love is an action, then serving others is a powerful demonstration of love. It also means that, like Christ, such service will personally cost us something. Life is not a "zero-sum game" – it never balances out. This is why God promises to reward us in eternity for the sacrificial life we live today.

So, don't be clueless like the original disciples, don't get caught up in the selfish culture of the world. Embrace the culture of the Kingdom, looking to the needs of others, knowing that in doing so there is a price to be paid. But Jesus promised it will be worth it!

Ask yourself these questions:

Am I living in the Kingdom culture while in the self-oriented culture of the world? Is my love for others actually being demonstrated in the real world?

Pray this prayer:

Father God, thank You for loving me and providing for my every physical, emotional and physical need through Your Son, Jesus Christ. Holy Spirit, empower me to love in and through my actions, caring for the needs of others even as I trust You to care for mine. I ask this in the name of the Father, and of the Son, and of the Holy Spirit. Amen.

Loving Others As You Love Yourself #2

by Dr. Tom Johnston

"I am a servant. I will love others with the love of Christ, seeking their welfare before my own."

Have this mind among yourselves, which is yours in Christ Jesus, who, though he was in the form of God, did not count equality with God a thing to be grasped, but emptied himself, by taking the form of a servant, being born in the likeness of men. (Philippians 2:5-7)

In addition to understanding our identity and vital to having a healthy and fruitful life is what I call capacity, and here is my "working definition":

Capacity: The inner state of being of a person – their nature, their character, their heart in the biblical sense, being enlarged by the work of the Holy Spirit unto the obedient service of God and the consequential loving embrace and service of others. (Johnston, Tom. The Way of the Master: The Leader Development Methodology of Jesus, p. 13. Kindle Edition.)

Identity is what gives us the security to live our life, to be confident and resolute in Christ. *Capacity* is the *heart of Christ's love in us* for other people. I am using the term capacity here not in the sense of *ability*, but rather as the *size of one's heart* for and towards others. It is through the work of the Holy Spirit that our heart grows to become more obedient to God and loving to others. Psalm 119:32 portrays this well*: "I will run in the way of your commandments when you enlarge my heart!"* We respond to God in loving obedience when we personally encounter His love and the resultant work of the Holy Spirit in us. We are actively, continually being "conformed to the image of his Son" (Romans 8:29a), the capacity of the heart to love with Christ's love is ever-increasing, ever-enlarging. This transformative work of the Spirit within us is essential to the fabric of our lives, as life itself is lived out in the context of relationships.

With *identity*, we understand ourselves as **sons and daughters** of God. With *capacity*, we embrace the **servant** heart of Jesus. The Apostle Paul's exhortation to the church at Philippi gives a broad understanding of how the servant heart of Jesus (*Phil. 2:5-7 above*) is meant to be expressed by and amongst His people:

> *So if there is any encouragement in Christ, any comfort from love, any participation in the Spirit, any affection and sympathy, complete my joy by being of the same mind, having the same love, being in full accord and of one mind. Do nothing from selfish ambition or conceit, but in humility count others more significant than yourselves. Let each of you look not only to his own interests, but also to the interests of others. (Philippians 2:1-4)*

Through this passage, Paul shows us the servanthood of Christ, who, as the Divine Son of God, chose *the humility of service*, even doing so by embracing a criminal's death. This is the "mind" we are to have within the Kingdom community in which we live and minister. We look at not only our needs but also those of others. We are not in competition with one another but are to esteem others as worthy of honor above ourselves. We seek their welfare; their needs being met before our own. As God stretches and enlarges our heart by the Holy Spirit to be like Christ, our capacity is increased. Such growth and transformation of our heart is critical for all disciples of Jesus. Kingdom life happens in the context of relationships. The nature of those relationships, whether healthy or unhealthy, is fundamental to the overall well-being of the Body and its missional fruitfulness.

My encouragement for you, dear fellow disciple, is to know your identity in Christ as a **son or daughter** and to encourage and invite His Holy Spirit to enlarge **the capacity of your heart**, that you might truly take on the servant role to which He has called you.

Ask yourself these questions:

How am I prioritizing the needs of others? Where is the Holy Spirit challenging me to serve others?

Pray this prayer:

Father God, thank You for sending Your Son, Jesus, to serve me through the Cross. Because of how He served me, I now have eternity with You. Holy Spirit, I ask that You enlarge my heart, empowering me for greater loving obedience to the Father and powerful, sacrificial service to others. Make my heart like the heart of Jesus, placing the needs of others before my own wants and desires. Make my heart whole, that I might love You and other people with my whole heart. I ask this in the name of the Father, and of the Son, and of the Holy Spirit. Amen.

Loving Others As You Love Yourself #3

by Tim McGinnin Jr.

"I am a servant. I will love others with the love of Christ, seeking their welfare before my own."

When he had washed their feet and put on his outer garments and resumed his place, he said to them, "Do you understand what I have done to you? You call me Teacher and Lord, and you are right, for so I am. If I then, your Lord and Teacher, have washed your feet, you also ought to wash one another's feet. For I have given you an example, that you also should do just as I have done to you. (John 13:12-15)

Jesus tells us outright in this Scripture that He is giving us an example to follow. The call to love one another through service is not unfamiliar in the Bible, and this account particularly is often cited to support living a way of life that embodies Christ's love for people. At the same time, it is easy to miss the significance of the moment between Jesus and His disciples. In this time, foot washing was a task reserved for the lowest household servant. It wasn't something that anyone would have wanted to do but something that needed to be done, so the menial and grimy task was given to the person of the lowest station in the home. Footwear primarily consisted of sandals and the roads and walkways were dirt and mud. People traveled the same roads as the animals and everything they expelled. To say that their feet would be filthy after a trip would be an immense understatement. In John's account (John 13:1-19), Jesus and the twelve sat down and began to eat but nobody had taken the time to wash everyone's feet upon arrival or prior to the meal as would have been normative and expected. Not one of the twelve was willing to take the place of a lowly servant in that moment. So, Jesus gets up in the middle of supper, fills a basin of water, grabs a towel to wrap around himself, and assumes the position of the lowliest servant on the floor as he washes the mud and muck from each of His disciples' feet.

He did not give us an example of service that comes easy to us. There are acts of service that we like to do. They are often the things that come naturally or don't require a whole lot of effort on our part, and they make us feel good. They make us feel like Christians. But Jesus invites us to serve in a much deeper way; the way He did...*to give of ourselves sacrificially, to elevate others high above ourselves, to put the needs of others well before our own.* Jesus' ultimate demonstration of love and service for us was accomplished on the cross where He died a physical death to bear our sins so that we wouldn't have to. *In His death for us, He calls us to die to ourselves and to serve others selflessly and sacrificially.* He calls us to get on the floor with a towel and do for others the things they wouldn't necessarily do for us. He calls us to give of ourselves to others in service because that is exactly what He did for us.

Ask yourself these questions:

How is the Lord inviting me to serve others sacrificially right now (this week)? What am I going to do about that?

Pray this prayer:

Lord, thank You for the sacrifice of Jesus on the cross! Thank You for demonstrating the living of a sacrificial life for me to live out with others. Holy Spirit, help me to love others the way Jesus does. Help me to serve others in tangible ways so that everyone around me will know that the love of Jesus Christ is real. Help me to die to myself in my desires and wants and to put others before myself. Help me to lay my life down, living for the benefit of those around me—just like You did. I ask this in the name of the Father, and of the Son, and of the Holy Spirit. Amen.

Loving Others As You Love Yourself #4

by Deryk Richenburg

"I am a servant. I will love others with the love of Christ, seeking their welfare before my own."

I am sending him back to you, sending my very heart. I would have been glad to keep him with me, in order that he might serve me on your behalf during my imprisonment for the gospel. (Philemon 1:12-13)

God brought Paul and Onesimus, a fugitive bondservant, together. They established a relationship and Paul led Onesimus to Christ and became his spiritual father (Philemon 1:10). Paul loved Onesimus dearly. Onesimus helped Paul personally and in the ministry.

Paul wrote in Philippians 2:4, "Let each of you look not only to his own interests, but also to the interests of others." That's the mindset Jesus had. Paul had it as well and he modeled it to Philemon and Onesimus. He thought of their interests before his own.

As Paul heard more of Onesimus' story, he knew the right thing to do would be to send Onesimus back to his owner, Philemon, so that they could be reconciled. This decision would cost Paul as Onesimus was personally beneficial to him. He could have justified keeping him reasoning that Paul's ministry was more important than Philemon's small house church.

Instead of thinking of himself and his ministry, Paul thought of Onesimus and Philemon. He knew they needed to be reconciled. He did all that he could to make that happen even when it wasn't best for Paul. He looked to their welfare before his own.

Each of us have decisions where we must choose between our own interests and the needs of others. For some it might be the decision to spend time with someone who is lonely instead of going home when you are tired. For others it might be to give some of the finances you were just given to someone who is in need. Often, we know the right thing to do but we get selfish. Paul chose to love others with the love of Christ.

Ask yourself this question:

When you think of others who are in "your ministry," are you helping them live out God's calling in their life or are you using them to do your ministry?

Pray this prayer:

Holy Spirit, would You transform me so that I have Jesus' mindset and think of the interests of others first. Speak loudly to me so that I might know how to help others like Paul helped Onesimus. In Jesus' name. Amen.

Loving Others As You Love Yourself #5

by John Kimball

"I am a servant. I will love others with the love of Christ, seeking their welfare before my own."

> *But Jesus called them to him and said, "You know that the rulers of the Gentiles lord it over them, and their great ones exercise authority over them. It shall not be so among you. But whoever would be great among you must be your servant, and whoever would be first among you must be your slave, even as the Son of Man came not to be served but to serve, and to give his life as a ransom for many. (Matthew 20:25-28)*

What started as a humorous story turned into an important lesson for all of us. We were on our first short-term missions trip in Japan and the missionary with whom we were working told us of a previous short-termer who complained about everything – including some things that were important to the Japanese culture. In the end, another team member finally responded to him, "Keep it up, 'cause you know this trip is all about you." He apparently got the message.

We had traveled literally halfway around the world to serve and to be witnesses to some of the most gracious people on earth. It was over 100 degrees and there was little air conditioning in most places. The rice patties had a peculiar smell. Some people were not doing well with the food we were provided. But none of these things really mattered. We were there to serve. And in the end, it was a successful ministry trip for Jesus' kingdom.

Western Christians often have a hard time with humility and serving others. But if we are truly going to be Christ-like, then service should be the norm. Jesus enjoyed glory, majesty and love with the Father and the Spirit from eternity past. Jesus is

King of all kings, and Lord of all lords. And yet He says, "*...the Son of Man did not come to be served, but to serve, and to give his life as a ransom for many.*" If Jesus, the Lord of glory, came to serve – and we are to be Christ-like – then we must be servants as well.

Ask yourself these questions:

In what ways do I resist humbly and joyfully serving those around me? And how will I overcome this?
Are there acts of service that I honestly think are beneath me? Why?
Do I find it challenging to serve certain people? If Jesus were serving beside me, would He be pleased with my attitude and my offering?
Do I notice the needs around me, offering to address them as I'm able?

Pray this prayer:

Jesus, thank You for Your sacrificial example. Thank You that You did not withhold service to us. Enable me by Your Holy Spirit to follow Your lead in humble service to those around me. Help me to serve people with genuine joy, and may that service always point to You and give You glory. Amen.

Loving Others As You Love Yourself #6

by Dr. Tom Johnston

"I will have a healthy appreciation of the self, based in my understanding of who I am in Christ."

See what kind of love the Father has given to us, that we should be called children of God; and so we are. (1 John 3:1a)

You would think that because God calls us His sons and daughters that we would have a better understanding of our own value as persons. However, too often that's just not the case. The voices from our own experiences in life can drown out the voice of God. The negative things which have been said to us and about us weigh heavily on our self-perception. Add to that the voice of the Adversary who always seeks to devalue God's image in the Earth – us. Having a healthy appreciation of who we are is super important, first, so we value what God has done for us in adopting us into His family through Christ, and second, that we be able to love and revalue others. It's really hard to love others when you don't really love yourself in Christ.

We also need to come to an awareness of how God's grace works through us (Romans 12:3). It is common for us to evaluate ourselves for sin, and appropriately so, that we might repent and be cleansed of it (1 John 1:9). However, we need also to *assess ourselves for grace*. We need to see the redeemed and transformed aspects of who we are, and rejoice in the work of the Holy Spirit in and through us. When we do, we can value the Lord in us, and we can be comfortable with who we are becoming in Christ. We value ourselves as His creation and as His new creation, honoring Him and enjoying who we are becoming in Him.

The Enemy will challenge you in your self-perception as a new creation in Christ. Hold fast to your identity as a child of God, and refuse the lies and condemnation of the Devil. Enjoy and rejoice in who you are becoming, yet don't be satisfied to remain where you are. Press onward and upward into who the Lord has always intended you to be!

Ask yourself these questions:

What are the lies about myself that I have been believing? What are some unique aspects of who I am becoming by God's grace?

Pray this prayer:

Father God, thank you for adopting me as your child. Holy Spirit, help me to understand and appreciate who I am in Christ. Reveal to me the amazing size of the Father's love for me, that in knowing it, I can share His love with others. I pray this in the name of the Father, and of the Son, and of the Holy Spirit. Amen.

Loving Others As You Love Yourself #7

by Dr. Tom Johnston

"I will have a healthy appreciation of the self, based in my understanding of who I am in Christ."

Did you know you have an enemy? You do – one who wants to hurt you, mar you – even kill every part of who you are:

> *Be sober-minded; be watchful. Your adversary the devil prowls around like a roaring lion, seeking someone to devour. Resist him, firm in your faith, knowing that the same kinds of suffering are being experienced by your brotherhood throughout the world. And after you have suffered a little while, the God of all grace, who has called you to his eternal glory in Christ, will himself restore, confirm, strengthen, and establish you. To him be the dominion forever and ever. Amen. (1 Peter 5:8-11)*

Because you bear the image of God – and the Enemy HATES God – he wants to corrupt you, hurt you – destroy you. Satan is desperately striking out at anything of God – and that includes *you*. He wants to *devalue you*, pulling down God's image, making you to be less than what the Father originally created you to be. The Good News is that this lion has no teeth, no real bite, as Jesus has already defeated him. The Lord has triumphed over the Devil and his demonic servants through the Cross and the Resurrection (ref. Colossians 2:15, Hebrews 2:14-15, 2 Timothy 1:10). As he has no teeth, *the Enemy works through lies*, weaving them into our hearts and minds, presenting us with a picture of ourselves which says we are unlovable, rejected and unwanted, worthless and fatherless. When we believe the Devil's lies, we align ourselves with them, and our actions and behaviors flow from this marred self-perception. In doing so we share the lie with others, bringing them down to our low estate through how we treat them.

The key to victory over lies is knowing the truth about who we are in Christ. Even as the Enemy seeks to *devalue us* and make us less, the Father through Christ has *revalued us*, bringing us into His family as beloved sons and daughters:

> *Blessed be the God and Father of our Lord Jesus Christ, who has blessed us in Christ with every spiritual blessing in the heavenly places, even as he chose us in him before the foundation of the world, that we should be holy and blameless before him. In love he predestined us for adoption to himself as sons through Jesus Christ, according to the purpose of his will, to the praise of his glorious grace, with which he has blessed us in the Beloved. In him we have redemption through his blood, the forgiveness of our trespasses, according to the riches of his grace, which he lavished upon us, in all wisdom and insight making known to us the mystery of his will, according to his purpose, which he set forth in Christ as a plan for the fullness of time, to unite all things in him, things in heaven and things on earth. (Ephesians 1:3-10)*

So, the truth is that:

> ***We are loved.***
> ***We are accepted.***
> ***We are desired.***
> ***We have been made worthy.***
> ***We do have a Father.***

When we *accept* the truth of who we are from God's perspective, we can *reject* the Enemy's lies and live out of the perspective of who we are in Christ. Then what we share with others out of our own lives is His love, acceptance and forgiveness. Through this we can revalue them as bearers of the Divine image, giving away what the Father has given us.

Ask yourself these questions:

DO I really believe what God has said about me? Where do I still believe the Enemy's lies about me?

Pray this prayer:

Father God, thank You for loving and accepting me through Christ. Holy Spirit, help me to accept the truth of who I am in Christ. Reveal to me where I still believe the lies of the Enemy, and replace those lies with the truth that I am loved, I am accepted, and that I do have a Father who desires and values me. I pray this in the name of the Father, and of the Son, and of the Holy Spirit. Amen.

Loving Others As You Love Yourself #8

By Tim McGinnin Jr.

"I will have a healthy appreciation of the self, based in my understanding of who I am in Christ."

For by the grace given to me I say to everyone among you not to think of himself more highly than he ought to think, but to think with sober judgment, each according to the measure of faith that God has assigned. (Romans 12:3)

In this Scripture, Paul is admonishing us not to be full of ourselves, not to think that we are more than we are. This is a good and important reminder for all of us. It keeps us humble. Yet, he is also saying that we are to think of ourselves clearly through the lens of how the Lord sees us. He wants us to see ourselves the way He created us to be. So, we shouldn't think too highly of ourselves, but then it would also imply that we shouldn't think too lowly of ourselves either. It is no mistake that this encouragement towards understanding our identity in Christ comes right after Paul appeals to us to live our entire lives as worship to the Lord and to seek the renewal of our minds in Him. It is only from this place of renewal in the Holy Spirit that we can understand who God has created us to be.

We think too highly of ourselves when we believe we have everything under control, when we are overly confident in our abilities to the point of neglecting a constant daily dependence on the Lord and realization of where He is at work in and through us, and when we place ourselves before God and others. We can see this play out in the Bible in many places, including with Jesus' twelve disciples who often vied for affirmation of positional value and sought places of importance and authority in eternity (cf. Mark 10:35-45). In contrast, we think too lowly of ourselves when we think that we can't accomplish anything of importance, that our lives have no impact or significance, and when we deny God's call on our lives and Spirit-given ability to fulfill His purposes for us.

Moses argued with God about his calling because he had difficulty with articulating his words and was slow in his speech (Exodus 4:10). The Lord's response to Moses is amazing in this interaction:

> *Then the LORD said to him, "Who has made man's mouth? Who makes him mute, or deaf, or seeing, or blind? Is it not I, the Lord? Now therefore go, and I will be with your mouth and teach you what you shall speak." (Exodus 4:11-12)*

God isn't concerned with our self-perceptions. When He calls us to do something, He is the one who accomplishes it in and through us. We must see ourselves as *fully dependent but completely empowered* sons and daughters of the living and all-powerful God who has *created us with a purpose that He can fulfill through us* if we give ourselves fully to Him and see ourselves the way He sees us.

Ask yourself these questions:

Do I have a tendency to view myself more highly than I ought or more lowly? How does my natural self-perception impact the way I relate to other people? How is the Lord inviting me to better understand who I am in Him?

Pray this prayer:

Lord, help me to see myself as You see me. Help me to understand who I am only through Your perspective. Show me where I see myself in a way that is not consistent with Your view of me. Forgive me for seeking to define and understand myself outside of my identity in You. Help me to walk obediently, knowing who I am so that I will

more fully love You and other people. I pray this in the name of the Father, and of the Son, and of the Holy Spirit. Amen.

Loving Others As You Love Yourself #9

by Deryk Richenburg

"I will have a healthy appreciation of the self, based in my understanding of who I am in Christ."

> *For we are His workmanship, created in Christ Jesus for good works, which God prepared beforehand, that we should walk in them. (Ephesians 2:10)*

For 25 years an enormous piece of marble remained neglected in the courtyard of Opera del Duomo in Florence, Italy. Two artists had tried to sculpt it but found that it had too many imperfections. Michelangelo created a masterpiece out of that "imperfect" marble known as "David."

Many times in our lives we feel like that neglected piece of marble. We don't fit the world's pattern. But that is not who you are – Jesus died for you and God created you into His magnificent work of art.

God says through Paul in Ephesians 2:10 that you are His masterpiece. The word Paul uses to describe you is the Greek word, *poiema,* from which we get the word poem. Different translations say we are His "masterpiece" (NLT), His "handiwork" (NAB), or His "work of art" (NJB).

Paul says that God is the artist and you are a custom-designed, tailor-made, divine work of art. He made you with gifts, talents, and strengths. He has worked in your life, putting you in places and relationships so that you gain knowledge and experience.

God created you this way because He has a purpose for you. He has "good works" that He wants you to do. He wants you to walk in them. He has given you everything you need, equipped you with tools, and fashioned you so that you are perfectly made to walk in those good works.

The world might discard you and say that you have too many

imperfections, but not God. He has made you into His masterpiece and you are far better than anything Michelangelo made. The question is: Do you believe it? Can you appreciate how God has made you or do you look for the world's affirmation?

Ask yourself these questions:

How has God made you? What gifts, talents, and strengths has He given you? How is He asking you to use them and walk in the good works He has set out before you?

Pray this prayer:

God, thank You for creating me in a unique way. Give me eyes to see what You see in me. Give me strength to live out of Your identity rather than the world's. In Jesus' name. Amen.

Loving Others As You Love Yourself #10

by Marjorie Clark

"I will have a healthy appreciation of the self, based in my understanding of who I am in Christ."

> *See what kind of love the Father has given to us, that we should be called children of God; and so we are. (1 John 3:1a)*

If you did a quick search to find the scriptures about loving your neighbor (Leviticus 19:18; Matthew 19:19; 22:39, Mark 12:31, Luke 10:27, Romans 13:9, Galatians 5:14, and James 2:8) you would discover that they all say the same thing. "Love your neighbor as yourself." We are not told, however, to love ourselves. It is assumed, and is closely related to what is known as the Golden Rule which we find in Matthew 7:12, "So whatever you wish that others would do to you, do also to them, for this is the Law and the Prophets." These Scriptures are based on the same assumption: we practice good self-care, we are kind to ourselves, we nurture and protect ourselves physically, psychologically, emotionally, and spiritually. Oh, that that were true of us all! Hence the prevailing dysfunction we see in our society.

If I do not have a healthy appreciation and care for myself, how can I possibly do the same for my child, my neighbor, my friend? I was created by God Almighty, the one who created all things, and by whom all things exist and *have their being* (Acts 17:28). Even when I was *dead in my sins* He made me alive through the death and resurrection of His Son and brought me *into* His family and legally and relationally made me His child! He calls me "daughter". That fills my heart and humbles me at the same time. As His child, I want to share all that He has given me with others – *especially with those who aren't yet in the family*! Because I've been given a place at the Table, I want everyone to have a place at the Table. Every time I look in the mirror, I see the one for whom Christ died. I see His love and grace, and I see that the woman looking back is one who has been chosen, called, and made worthy to bring His love to the world in which I am an alien and a sojourner.

I know who I was, and I know who I am now, and that is the basis for the first thing I say every morning when my eyes open, "Good morning, Father!"

Ask yourself these questions:

We believe many things about ourselves that are not true – what lies have you believed? What is the truth that God says about you? How will you replace the lies with the truth?

Pray this prayer:

Father, thank you for making me Your child! I confess that I don't always believe the truth about my identity, but have sought validation from others, from my talents and education and achievements. And yet, that is never enough. I am complete in You. I want to wake up every day thinking of You and looking forward to the great adventure of walking with You, hand in hand, as we take the good news of Your love to the world. I am blessed to be Your child. I will rejoice in who You made me to be and I choose to see myself as You see me. You are the joy of my heart! Amen.

Loving Others As You Love Yourself #11

by Dr. Tom Johnston

"I will seek self-awareness through God-awareness."

For now we see in a mirror dimly, but then face to face. Now I know in part; then I shall know fully, even as I have been fully known. (1 Corinthians 13:12)

There will come a day when we fully understand who we are. That day will be when we see Jesus face-to-face. But in the here-and-now we can grow in our understanding of who we are. This happens as we go deeper into our relationship with Father God. Our Creator is the only one who knows us, and the only one who can help us know ourselves.

The more we encounter Him, the more we encounter our true self. Our human sin and brokenness are revealed as well has His grace at work in us. Through this revelation He leads us to repentance, and He leads us to greater works. Through knowing Him we are transformed, and can function in the grace upon our lives:

I appeal to you therefore, brothers, by the mercies of God, to present your bodies as a living sacrifice, holy and acceptable to God, which is your spiritual worship. Do not be conformed to this world, but be transformed by the renewal of your mind, that by testing you may discern what is the will of God, what is good and acceptable and perfect. For by the grace given to me I say to everyone among you not to think of himself more highly than he ought to think, but to think with sober judgment, each according to the measure of faith that God has assigned. (Romans 12:1-3)

Through our knowledge of Him and knowing ourselves, we are empowered to love others. The more we know His love for us the more we love Him in return, and the more that love flows out to others. In knowing ourselves we can be mindful of our own brokenness and how it impacts our relationships, and in knowing our grace we can understand how we have been shaped to love and serve others. When we know ourselves, and know that we are loved by Him, it becomes easy to love others.

Ask yourself these questions:

What am I doing to know God more? What am I learning about me? How am I sharing the love He has given me by serving others?

Pray this prayer:

Father God may I know You more fully, that I might know who I am more completely. Holy Spirit, help me understand myself in such a way as it leads me to loving and serving others – even has God has loved and served me in Christ. I pray this in the name of the Father, and of the Son, and of the Holy Spirit. Amen.

Loving Others As You Love Yourself #12

by Dr. Tom Johnston

"I will seek self-awareness through God-awareness."

> *But by the grace of God I am what I am, and his grace toward me was not in vain. On the contrary, I worked harder than any of them, though it was not I, but the grace of God that is with me. (1 Corinthians 15:10)*

We live out of the framework of the understanding of who we are. Our definition leads to our doing. Accordingly, understanding who we are from God's perspective – as we have discussed, it is our Creator who defines us – is really important to our everyday lives. When we don't know who we are we live incorrectly from God's perspective. Without knowing who we are, we are unable to "walk in a manner worthy of the calling to which you have been called." (Ephesians 4:1) In other words, we cannot live in alignment with God's purposes and intention for our lives.

The Apostle Paul said that it was God's grace which empowered and defined him, and that how he lived and served Jesus was based on this grace. Now, *grace* is more than "forgiveness" or "mercy," although both come to us because of God's grace. Grace defined is God's *unmerited favor*, His approval which we did not earn. It has the imagery of someone laying their hand on another as a sign of *being chosen by the person's own will*, not by it having been earned. Paul understood himself from the perspective of God's choosing, not his earning. He understood that it was God's choosing that empowered him to live for Christ, and to serve Him. Paul was aware of God and His work in his life, and through this knew who he was as someone who had been chosen and empowered by Him. His awareness of His Creator made him aware of who he was.

Like Paul, each of us who follow Christ have been chosen by

Him. And Like Paul, we too have received God's unmerited favor through placing our trust in King Jesus. As we also accept His definition of who we are as sons and daughters of the Most High, we can live from the place of our acceptance in Christ. The more we know Him, the more we know ourselves – and the more we can truly know others. The more we know ourselves in Him, the more fully we *"walk in a manner worthy of the calling to which you have been called."* Seek to know the Father's definition of you, which is something that you have not earned, but which has been accorded to you by His grace.

Ask yourself these questions:

Who am I, really? Am I still trying to earn God's favor, or have I simply accepted that I already have it in Christ?

Pray this prayer:

Father God, I accept who You made me to be. Thank You for choosing me. Holy Spirit, help me to surrender my understanding of myself. Open my heart and mind to truly know who I am in You. I pray this in the name of the Father, and of the Son, and of the Holy Spirit. Amen.

Loving Others As You Love Yourself #13

by Tim McGinnin Jr.

"I will seek self-awareness through God-awareness."

Search me, O God, and know my heart! Try me and know my thoughts! And see if there be any grievous way in me and lead me in the way everlasting! (Psalm 139:23-24)

David's prayer in Psalm 139 is all about aligning with what God already knows. When he asks the Lord to search him and know his heart, it is not as if God doesn't already know everything, nor does David think that He doesn't. In verse 1 he says, "O Lord, you have searched me and known me!" He starts off by acknowledging that God already knows everything about him. More than that, he is aware that it is the Lord who created and formed him, even when he was still in his mother's womb and even before that, He already understood every facet of what David's life would look like from beginning to end (v. 13, 16). The closing statements of "search me" and "know my thoughts" are about David seeking to become aware of himself as God is already aware of him. God cannot know David more than He already does because His knowledge and understanding of him is already perfect and complete. David is petitioning the Lord to reveal the things within himself that he doesn't even know about himself so that he might walk in the way of the Lord by coming to a greater sense of self-awareness through God-awareness.

Self-awareness is not just of personal benefit for us, but it is also an incredibly important quality to have to be in healthy and loving relationships with other people. The most self-aware people are those who attain self-awareness through God-awareness. The Lord knows us fully and completely, so the more we seek Him and know Him, the more He reveals Himself to us; and the more He reveals ourselves to us as well. The more we understand ourselves through God's awareness of us, the better we are able understand what it is like to be on the other side of ourselves in the relationships we have. When I ask the Lord to reveal my own heart to me, I am asking Him to show me all my sin and imperfection so that I might repent and live more fully unto Him. When I am doing this and responding to His leading, I am a better husband, father, son, brother, co-worker, neighbor, and so on. When my own self-awareness is informed by God's awareness and knowledge of me, I am better equipped to live out the Irreducible Core of loving God, loving others, and making disciples everywhere I go.

Ask yourself these questions:

How has my self-awareness impacted my relationships with others, positively and negatively? How is the Lord inviting me to become more aware of myself through His knowledge and understanding of me? What is He trying to show me about me right now?

Pray this prayer:

Lord, search my heart and reveal it to me. Show me the blind spots that I have about myself so that I can more fully align with Your will for me. Forgive me when I have sinned against You and others and lead me in Your way so that You might be glorified in all that I do. Help me to be aware of myself as You are aware of me. I pray this in the name of the Father, and of the Son, and of the Holy Spirit. Amen.

Loving Others As You Love Yourself #14

by Selina McGinnin

"I will seek self-awareness through God-awareness."

We've all been called many things. Some of those things we are proud of and some we would rather forget. Typically, the ones we would rather forget are ones that have left scars and in some cases trauma. Often what others call us can become our identity, we become who those around us say we are. Proud, dumb, insignificant, silly, foolish, smart, strong, weak, forgettable, a screw up, and the list goes on. As we read in 2 Corinthians, we learn that Paul also knew something about this.

> *Look at what is before your eyes. If anyone is confident that he is Christ's, let him remind himself that just as he is Christ's, so also are we. For even if I boast a little too much of our authority, which the Lord gave for building you up and not for destroying you, I will not be ashamed. I do not want to appear to be frightening you with my letters. For they say, "His letters are weighty and strong, but his bodily presence is weak, and his speech of no account." Let such a person understand that what we say by letter when absent, we do when present. Not that we dare to classify or compare ourselves with some of those who are commending themselves. But when they measure themselves by one another and compare themselves with one another, they are without understanding. (2 Corinthians 10:7-12)*

The church at Corinth was trying to discredit Paul's ministry. They called him weak and criticized his ability to speak. They essentially were calling him two-faced for acting one way in his letters and not appearing that way in person. Did you notice Paul's response? He reminded both himself and the people accusing him that they all belong to Christ and to regard one another that way (v7). He recalled that his authority was given to him by the Lord (v8) so he would not be ashamed. Lastly, he called out their comparison, saying to measure and compare themselves by one another would be unwise (v12).

Paul knew who he was because he knew who God was. He knew God's purpose for him and he knew where his value and identity came from – Christ. He knew better than to compare himself to others, because others did not define him or measure him. It was this wisdom that kept Paul in alignment with God's will and purposes for his life. The outcome of that life lived was many knowing about the Gospel and believing in Jesus. Our self-awareness is never just for ourselves but influences those around us.

We too will face people like those in Corinth and we too must become secure in our identity and who God says we are like Paul did. The more we know about God the more we know about ourselves and the less movable and more secure we become.

Ask yourself these questions:

What have I believed about myself because someone said it or treated me that way? Who am I comparing myself to and why?

What is God saying about me and calling me to? (Hint: If you don't know what God says about you, read: Ephesians 2:10, John 1:12, Galatians 4:7, Ephesians 1:4 & 7, 1 Thessalonians 1:4)

Pray this prayer:

Father, thank You I am known by You. My identity can only be found in You and no one else. Lord, forgive me where I have accepted as my identity what other people have thought of me over who You have made me to be. Please remove the effects on me of these comparisons and words spoken over me in Jesus' name. Begin to make me whole and help me to see myself the way You see me, Lord. Thank you for Your defining love, God.

Amen.

Loving Others As You Love Yourself #15

by Marjorie Clark

"I will seek self-awareness through God-awareness."

For now we see in a mirror dimly, but then face to face. Now I know in part; then I shall know fully, even as I have been fully known. (I Corinthians 13:12)

Several years ago, a wonderful tradition began in our family. On your birthday, after the cake and other goodies, everyone – family and friends, children and adults – gathered around to bless you. In no particular order, each one would share what you meant to them, what they saw and appreciated in you, and what they perceived of your future as you looked forward to a new year of life. Gratitude, value, vision, a 'becoming' ... all brings joy and laughter and connection. The people in our lives are a mirror to us – reflecting back what they see. It's not a perfect picture, but it's often a clearer picture than what we see of ourselves as most of us are insecure and uncertain and self-critical when we 'look in the mirror'. Those birthday blessings are the best gift of all. I don't know how many of the spoken words I recall from the times when I was the 'birthday girl' but I do recall having an overwhelming sense of being seen, loved, and valued. I knew I was making a difference in lives even if I sometimes failed.

There's another aspect as well. As we would all share in this time of blessing, we were aware that the good that we saw in each other was the Christ we saw in each other. We truly are made in His image. I think that's why the gospels are so precious to me and always a part of my reading. I see Jesus – His devotion to His Father, His love for all people, His certainty in Who He was and what He was here to do – and the more I see and hear Him, the more I become like Him because He lives in me by His Spirit.

Let's keep our focus fixed on Jesus, the author and finisher of our faith (Hebrews 12:2) that we might be transformed into His image as we see and worship Him only. Let's be mirrors to one another – reflecting the image of Christ – speaking into people's lives the goodness of Jesus we see reflected in them (even if it's not yet fully developed).

Ask yourself these questions:

Who are the mirrors in my life who see Jesus in me and encourage me? Who can I encourage in the same way? In what area of my life do I want to look more like Jesus?

Pray this prayer:

Father, I want to be more and more like Jesus. Please forgive me for my own critical voice of comparison and show me, tell me, what You see when You look at me. I know You know me fully and love me unconditionally. Thank you for Your love. I'm asking that you continue to work in me to make me more and more like the person You created me to be. I'm asking this in Jesus' name. **Amen.** (*Pause and listen to the Lord, reflecting on what He is saying to you.*)

Loving Others As You Love Yourself #16

by Dr. Tom Johnston

"Loving and serving others is my second priority."

So if there is any encouragement in Christ, any comfort from love, any participation in the Spirit, any affection and sympathy, complete my joy by being of the same mind, having the same love, being in full accord and of one mind. Do nothing from selfish ambition or conceit, but in humility count others more significant than yourselves. Let each of you look not only to his own interests, but also to the interests of others. (Philippians 2:1-4)

Sometimes it's really hard to serve others. I mean, really serve, not just the occasional helping-hand when it is convenient. The needs people have often arise in the most inopportune moments. In our flesh we may feel annoyed or bothered when we have to respond to something someone else needs. We are busy enough with our own things: work, family, running errands, and our regular life-maintenance tasks. Yet, the Scripture challenges our self-focus and points us to the example of Christ who gave Himself for us on the Cross:

Have this mind among yourselves, which is yours in Christ Jesus, who, though he was in the form of God, did not count equality with God a thing to be grasped, but emptied himself, by taking the form of a servant, being born in the likeness of men. And being found in human form, he humbled himself by becoming obedient to the point of death, even death on a cross. (Philippians 2:5-8)

Through the transforming work of the Holy Spirit, we are led to prioritize the needs of others before our own. The things we may want or think we need are entrusted to Christ, with our focus instead being on those around us: natural and spiritual family, friends, co-workers – and the occasional random stranger. Because of Christ, we must allow our lives to be interrupted and reprioritized around caring for others. Remember, love is not just and emotion – *it's an action.* Love which is demonstrated in real and powerful ways, even as the Cross was a very real demonstration of the Father's love for us. Shift your focus – make loving others in practical action your second priority.

Ask yourself these questions:

Where is my selfishness impacting my relationships? Who do I need to be more actively serving – and how?

Pray this prayer:

Father God give me the servant heart of Jesus. I trust You to care for my needs. Holy Spirit, I ask You to continue to guide me to those You would have me serve, regularly and consistently. I pray this in the name of the Father, and of the Son, and of the Holy Spirit. Amen.

Loving Others As You Love Yourself #17

by Tim McGinnin Jr.

"Loving and serving others is my second priority."

> *By this we know love, that he laid down his life for us, and we ought to lay down our lives for the brothers. But if anyone has the world's goods and sees his brother in need, yet closes his heart against him, how does God's love abide in him? Little children, let us not love in word or talk but in deed and in truth. (1 John 3:16-18)*

The church historian Jerome records that when the apostle John was very old in age, he was so physically weak that his disciples would carry him to church gatherings. He did not often have the strength to say a whole lot in these environments, but when he did speak, he would say nothing but "little children, love one another." Expecting a much deeper utterance from one of the twelve that walked with Jesus, those in attendance would get annoyed and ask him why he would always only repeat this one statement. His response: "Because it is the Lord's commandment and if it alone is kept, it is sufficient." The significance and profundity of this simple statement has enduring implications for followers of Jesus.

John, who referred to himself as the "disciple whom Jesus loved" in his own Gospel account, was apparently enamored with the love of Jesus and how that love was to overflow out of His followers towards others. We see it come through in his letters as described in the Scripture above. This man who walked with Jesus during his earthly ministry and continued to do so empowered by the Holy Spirit for the rest of his life had truly embraced Jesus' command to love God and love others (see Matthew 22:34-40). He knew how inseparable those two things truly are. When we read on in his first letter, he says that "God is love" (1

John 4:8b) and that our very ability to love comes from the fact that "he first loved us" (1 John 4:19). He would repeat his mantra about loving one another to the very end of his life because he knew that it was the essence of what it meant to live our lives fully submitted to the Lord.

If we love God first with everything that we are and everything we have; if that is indeed our first priority, then what will immediately follow is loving others. We will love authentically, deeply, and sacrificially. This is how Christ loved us, and it is from that place of being loved that we are called to love one another.

Ask yourself these questions:

How has God's love for me poured out into love for others in real and tangible ways? How is the Lord inviting me to grow in my love for other people?

Pray this prayer:

Loving and gracious Father, thank You for loving me so sacrificially and completely! Help me to better understand and embrace the love that You have for me so that it does indeed pour out of me into the lives of other people. Help me to love everyone around me the way You love so that they might encounter You through me. I pray this in the name of the Father, and of the Son, and of the Holy Spirit. Amen.

Loving Others As You Love Yourself #18

by Dr. Tom Johnston

"Loving and serving others is my second priority."

So, if you are going to serve people it will cost some of your precious time. I've heard it said "time is worth more than money," and it's often true. Yet it is part of our calling as disciples of Jesus that we serve others sacrificially, like He served us on the Cross.

Serving others will take your time. It requires that you be in the same space and time as someone else as you care for whatever it is that they need. At the least, it will be that you have to carve out a chunk of your day to address the situations or problems that others may face. The needs of others are rarely convenient, as they often push back against other things we would like to do with our time. Even when we do make the time, we need to guard ourselves against taking a minimalist approach, as Jesus taught us to go over, above, and beyond the basics of what others ask (or even force) us to do:

> *And if anyone would sue you and take your tunic, let him have your cloak as well. And if anyone forces you to go one mile, go with him two miles. Give to the one who begs from you, and do not refuse the one who would borrow from you. (Matthew 5:40-42)*

Wow, that's amazing! We may even be asked to serve those who make unreasonable demands on us and our time! Paul in writing to the church in Galatia, indicated that someone's need is an *opportunity to do good*:

> *And let us not grow weary of doing good, for in due season we will reap, if we do not give up. So then, as we have opportunity, let us do good to everyone, and especially to those who are of the household of faith. (Galatians*

6:9-10)

However the need arises, we need to be willing to give our time. It may be a single instance of helping someone, or it might be where we are called upon to consistently give of our time to someone who needs our help. It's an opportunity to do good, to emulate Jesus and demonstrate His love. So, better make room in your schedule, as God has people right around you who need your time.

Ask yourself these questions:

Do I overly protect my time from the needs of others? Who needs me right now?

Pray this prayer:

Father God, give me the servant heart of Jesus. Holy Spirit, open my eyes to see the needs of the people right around me, and show me how I am currently wasting time which would be better invested in meeting the needs of others. I pray this in the name of the Father, and of the Son, and of the Holy Spirit. Amen.

Loving Others As You Love Yourself #19

by Dr. Tom Johnston

"Loving and serving others is my second priority."

When I was a kid, I learned to play the drums and when I got into high school and college, I started to play with other people, trying to form rock bands. Alas, none of these turned out to be anything, and my dreams of being a rock star died a quick and early death. The truth was, I wasn't a very good drummer, and by the end of college I sold my set and moved on into married life.

About four years after we got married, my wife Cathy and I got involved with a new church plant. One of our new friends in the church was Mike, and he became one of the worship leaders. And yes, you guessed it, he asked me to play the drums on the worship team. Now, remember, I said I wasn't very good – it was true – and I knew it. So, I originally told him no, as I really hadn't played in years, and didn't want to look ridiculous on a Sunday morning in front of the congregation. But as the church was still small and was in need of someone to play, he was persistent in asking me. Finally, I said to him in jest, "Well, if you get down on your knees and beg me to play, I will," thinking the whole time there was no way he would do that. But in similar humor, he did just that. I was stuck. He got me, so I gave in and started to play with the team. At first, I dreaded it, but the Lord gave me a grace for it, and people seemed to be blessed by it. I did it for several years, and then a guy came along who was a professional grade drummer, and I was able to step aside. By then, Mike was okay with me doing so – I think he had enough of my erratic tempo. (Side note: more than 20 years later, the new guy became the drummer in a church I pastored! I guess you do reap what you sow!)

I wasn't called to be a rock star, or a worship team drummer, I was called to be a pastor. *But when the need arose, I had a talent that would be helpful for a season.* I know that many people think they have nothing to give in service to others, but that couldn't be further from the truth. Every Christian has something of Jesus to bring to the table in service of others. Natural ability, talents, spiritual gifts, acquired skills – whatever it is, we should use it to help others:

> *To each is given the manifestation of the Spirit for the common good. (1 Corinthians 12:7)*
>
> *As each has received a gift, use it to serve one another, as good stewards of God's varied grace. (1 Peter 4:10)*

We all have things we can do to help people, to build the Body of Christ. Can you cook? Then feed people. In the New Testament, people were always eating together! Are you hospitable? Then open your home and create an environment for God to work in people's lives. Can you fix things? People have lots of broken stuff. Can you play the drums? Do it, because you really don't want me to! Can you teach, share the Scripture with people hungry to learn. Do you prophesy? Share the encouraging word of the Lord with people who need it.

Don't waste your gifts and other abilities on things that do not build God's Kingdom. Prioritize the investment of your abilities in the things of God, those things which move people forward in their relationship with Jesus. Don't hold back, press beyond your fear, and whatever you do, don't make somebody get down on their knees and beg for your help. Just do it!

Ask yourself these questions:

What skills, gifts and abilities has God given me? Am I using them for the benefit others?

Pray this prayer:

Father God, help me to know how to use what You have given me in talents, skills, abilities and spiritual gifts for You, Your Church, and Your mission. Holy Spirit, open my eyes to see the needs right around me that You have designed me to meet. Show me how I am currently wasting my talents on other things which are not aligned to Your Kingdom. I pray this in the name of the Father, and of the Son, and of the Holy Spirit. Amen.

Loving Others As You Love Yourself #20

by Dr. Tom Johnston

"Loving and serving others is my second priority."

On Sunday, when someone is receiving the offering as part of our worship celebration, I often hear people say, "God doesn't need your money." Well, this is true from a certain perspective. What He needs is HIS money, and by the way, you have it. Settle that right now – everything you are and everything you have has come from Him, and belongs to Him. The financial resources you have are not yours, they are His – you and I are just stewards of those resources. We attend to them and administrate them, moving them to the places He needs them to be. And very often, that place is in someone else's pocket.

We know that God is the *source* of our own provision:

> *Beware lest you say in your heart, 'My power and the might of my hand have gotten me this wealth.' You shall remember the LORD your God, for it is he who gives you power to get wealth, that he may confirm his covenant that he swore to your fathers, as it is this day. (Deuteronomy 8:17-18)*

Likewise, the Lord uses us as the means of provision for others in their moment of need:

> *He who supplies seed to the sower and bread for food will supply and multiply your seed for sowing and increase the harvest of your righteousness. You will be enriched in every way to be generous in every way, which through us will produce thanksgiving to God. For the ministry of this service is not only supplying the needs of the saints but is also overflowing in many thanksgivings to God. By their approval of this service, they will glorify God because of*

your submission that comes from your confession of the gospel of Christ, and the generosity of your contribution for them and for all others. (2 Corinthians 9:10-13)

Financial resources exist for one reason – *God meeting the needs of people.* That includes us, as well as the others He directs us to help. We need to prioritize our finances in such a way that we are always ready to respond when needs arise. And it may be that we do so in a sacrificial manner, giving not out of our surplus, but rather caring for others while we ourselves still have need. Rees Howells, the great intercessor of the Welsh revival in the early 20th Century had a concept of "*first need, first claim.*" In other words, whoever he knew had the immediate need had the first claim on his resources. In certain times he would even give people funds which he had laid aside for an upcoming need, only to be provided for himself through some miraculous means. He trusted the Lord so much that he prioritized the needs of others, knowing God would take care of him.

This should be our heart as well. Even as we trust the Lord to provide for us, we need to be available to Him as His vehicle of provision to others in need. Remember, you can never outgive God!

Ask yourself these questions:

Do I really prioritize the needs of others? Do I truly see God as my source of provision?

Pray this prayer:

Father God, thank You for the financial provision You have made available to me. Holy Spirit, help me use it wisely, and show me who You would have me serve as a means of Your provision. I pray this in the name of the Father, and of the Son, and of the Holy Spirit. Amen.

AS YOU GO, MAKING DISCIPLES

(Matthew 28:18-20)

"I am a steward. My mission as a disciple of Jesus Christ is to make more and better disciples for Him everywhere I go. It is the outworking of my loving devotion to Christ and His Church." ***(Matthew 28:18-20)***

"I will be a witness who shares with others the comfort that I myself have received from God through Jesus Christ." ***(Acts 1:8, 2 Corinthians 1:3-5, John 9:25)***

"Making disciples is my third priority."

As You Go, Making Disciples #1

by Dr. Tom Johnston

"I am a steward. My mission as a disciple of Jesus Christ is to make more and better disciples for Him everywhere I go. It is the outworking of my loving devotion to Christ and His Church."

In two previous devotionals, I offered elements of a core construct of our redeemed personhood – identity and capacity – and how these elements of who we are in Christ are foundational to the functioning of our leadership. I laid out how leadership flows from inside us to those around us. It comes from our very being and is not just a task or role we play. I shared how I see leadership as influence and how Christ uses the totality of our redeemed personhood as the means of such effect.

Our identity in Christ gives us the security to live for and be confident and determined in Him. Capacity is the heart of Christ's love for those whom we lead. In our identity, we are *sons and daughters* (ref. John 1:12). In our capacity, we are *servants* called to care for the needs of others, embracing them as Jesus would (ref. Psalm 119:32, Philippians 2:1-11). These are fundamental elements of who we are and the associated relational roles out of which we lead.

Today, I'd like to introduce another core construct built upon our identity and capacity and which is essential to our healthy and fruitful life in the Kingdom way of Jesus. It is something which I have named as *destiny*, and here is my "working definition":

> ***Destiny:*** *The unique Kingdom contribution an individual makes through partnering with God in the co-creative process of expressing dominion. It is the expression of God's creative nature in the person, manifesting in the form of valued relational roles and uniquely specific tasks within God's Kingdom economy. (Johnston, Tom. The Way of the Master: The Leader Development Method-*

ology of Jesus. (2021), p. 14. Kindle Edition.)

As I have defined it, *destiny* is the particular impact that we have within God's Kingdom endeavor as we partner with Him in His mission. There is something of Jesus, unique in each of us, that is His expression through us. Only you can be you in Christ. Only you can do what He has called you to do. No one else can make the contribution to His "Kingdom economy" that is yours alone to make. Yes, that's right – there is something of Jesus only you can bring to the table. And if you don't, well, we are lessened, the Body of Christ impacted, and the mission of God impaired. We need Jesus in you; we need you to fulfill your destiny!

In our *identity,* we are **sons and daughters.** In our *capacity* of heart, we are **servants**. In our *destiny*, we are **stewards** who hold *a place of responsibility in the Kingdom.* The grace upon our lives is a valued investment by God in us, and we must use it for His purposes and for His glory. Stewardship is taking responsibility for something that is not our own and using it to benefit the one who does own it. We were bought with a price, the precious blood of Jesus. We are not our own (ref. 1 Corinthians 6:20; 7:23). Jesus tells many parables about our stewardship responsibility in the Scripture. One parable of note which many are familiar with concerns the Talents, and is found in Matthew 25:14-30:

> *"For it will be like a man going on a journey, who called his servants and entrusted to them his property. To one he gave five talents, to another two, to another one, to each according to his ability. Then he went away. He who had received the five talents went at once and traded with them, and he made five talents more. So also he who had the two talents made two talents more. But he who had received the one talent went and dug in the ground and hid his master's money. Now after a long time the master of those servants came and settled accounts with them. And he who had received the five talents came forward, bringing five talents more, saying, 'Master, you delivered*

to me five talents; here, I have made five talents more.' His master said to him, 'Well done, good and faithful servant. You have been faithful over a little; I will set you over much. Enter into the joy of your master.' And he also who had the two talents came forward, saying, 'Master, you delivered to me two talents; here, I have made two talents more.' His master said to him, 'Well done, good and faithful servant. You have been faithful over a little; I will set you over much. Enter into the joy of your master.' He also who had received the one talent came forward, saying, 'Master, I knew you to be a hard man, reaping where you did not sow, and gathering where you scattered no seed, so I was afraid, and I went and hid your talent in the ground. Here, you have what is yours.' But his master answered him, 'You wicked and slothful servant! You knew that I reap where I have not sown and gather where I scattered no seed? Then you ought to have invested my money with the bankers, and at my coming I should have received what was my own with interest. So take the talent from him and give it to him who has the ten talents. For to everyone who has will more be given, and he will have an abundance. But from the one who has not, even what he has will be taken away. And cast the worthless servant into the outer darkness. In that place there will be weeping and gnashing of teeth.'

The King is looking for a return on His investment in us. There is an expectation to "trade" and "invest" what He has placed in us. He is looking for the multiplication of His Kingdom life through us in proportion to what He has given us. Christ's calling upon us, the Holy Spirit at work through us, comes with the expectation of fruitfulness. Our roles within that calling need to align with and be empowered by His gifts. Our best contribution comes, our destiny is fulfilled, when our grace-gifts and assignment align. We must not allow ourselves to either waste His investment in us through inaction or disengagement, nor spend what we have been given on efforts outside the bounds of our gifting. We must hit the "niche" He has for us if we are going to fully engage our destiny.

As you can see, discovering one's God-originated destiny is crucial in our holistic approach to understanding human personhood *and* is absolutely essential for leaders to be effective in their calling. As Thomas Merton noted:

> *Each one of us has some kind of vocation. We are all called by God to share in His life and in His Kingdom. If we find that place we will be happy. If we do not find it, we can never be completely happy. For each one of us, there is only one thing necessary: to fulfill our own destiny, according to God's will, to be what God wants us to be (Merton, Thomas. No Man is an Island (2003), p. 131).*

So, dear brothers and sisters, have you found your place of Kingdom contribution that matches and fits your calling and current gifts? Perhaps there is a long way to go in your development before the ultimate contribution to the Kingdom can be made. That's alright – serve where you are now. Make what contribution you can. Grow in your grace, learn to wear it, to flow with it, and to move in it. Be a blessing now. Seek to grow in your identity, your capacity, and your understanding of your grace-gifts, that you might grow into – and fulfill God's intended purposes for you. What He has called you to do has been prepared beforehand – you just need to walk it out with Him. It is your destiny!

> *For by grace you have been saved through faith. And this is not your own doing; it is the gift of God, not a result of works, so that no one may boast. For we are his workmanship, created in Christ Jesus for good works, which God prepared beforehand, that we should walk in them. (Ephesians 2:8-10)*

Ask yourself these questions:

Am I being responsible with God's investment of Christ in me? How am I walking in the good works He has prepared for me?

Pray this prayer:

Father God, help me to discover and realize the purpose for which You made me. Holy Spirit, help me to know and actualize all the grace-gifts You have empowered me with. Lead me in the path of discovery of all the good works that You have already prepared for me to do as I walk with You through life. May I become a blessing to others, and may I be useful to You in making more and better disciples for Jesus, every day of my life, everywhere I go. I ask this in the name of the Father, and of the Son, and of the Holy Spirit. Amen.

As You Go, Making Disciples #2

by Dr. Tom Johnston

"I am a steward. My mission as a disciple of Jesus Christ is to make more and better disciples for Him everywhere I go. It is the outworking of my loving devotion to Christ and His Church."

Stewardship is about being responsible with something which is not our own. Many of Jesus' parables were about the oikonomos, which is the ancient Greek word for steward or household manager. Jesus is looking for us to be attentive to the stewardship He has given to us:

> *And the Lord said, "Who then is the faithful and wise manager, whom his master will set over his household, to give them their portion of food at the proper time? Blessed is that servant whom his master will find so doing when he comes. Truly, I say to you, he will set him over all his possessions." (Luke 12:42–44)*

He is looking for us to discharge the duties which He has assigned to us with all effort – using whatever He has given us in talent, abilities, financial resources, etc. -- all for the work of His Kingdom. We are to apply ourselves, everything we are and everything we have, to making more and better disciples for Him, everywhere we go, all the time. What that looks like will be different from person to person, as we each have a different expression of His grace which shines through us:

> *As each has received a gift, use it to serve one another, as good stewards of God's varied grace: whoever speaks, as one who speaks oracles of God; whoever serves, as one who serves by the strength that God supplies—in order that in everything God may be glorified through Jesus Christ. To him belong glory and dominion forever and ever. Amen. (1 Peter 4:10-11)*

You have something of Jesus invested *in you* that He might make disciples *through you*. Remember, *"You are not your own, for you were bought with a price."* (1 Corinthians 6:19b-20a) Invest yourself in the things of God, and by so doing, fulfill your responsibility as His steward!

Ask yourself these questions:

How am I currently taking responsibility for making disciples? AM I using who I am and what I have to advance His Kingdom?

Pray this prayer:

Father God, thank You for investing in me and trusting me as a steward in the household of God. Holy Spirit, led and guide me in using who I am and what I have to see more people become disciples of Jesus. I ask this in the name of the Father, and of the Son, and of the Holy Spirit. Amen.

As You Go, Making Disciples #3

by Tim McGinnin Jr.

"I am a steward. My mission as a disciple of Jesus Christ is to make more and better disciples for Him everywhere I go. It is the outworking of my loving devotion to Christ and His Church."

> *Or do you not know that your body is a temple of the Holy Spirit within you, whom you have from God? You are not your own, for you were bought with a price. So glorify God in your body. (1 Corinthians 6:19-20)*

There is something about the statement "you are not your own" that grates against my flesh. There is a part of me that immediately wants to defy that scriptural truth. "What do you mean I'm not my own? Of course I am! I have a free will. I make my own decisions." In modern Western culture, we are taught to be our own person; to be independent; to define our own truths and our own selves. A marker of success in the world is to make your own way and to do whatever you want to do. This approach to life, however, does not align with the Kingdom of God. Success in the Kingdom of God is to deny the self and to be radically obedient to the Lord. In the Kingdom, we are not our own people. We are sons and daughters of the living God by the blood of Jesus; fully created and completely defined by Him alone. We are to be wholly dependent on Him for every aspect of our lives, to live interdependently with others in community, even as we journey through life making "more and better disciples" by the power of the Holy Spirit working in and through us.

When we choose to be in relationship with the Lord, *we give up our right to define ourselves*. We fully surrender our whole lives to Him and we become the dwelling place of the Holy Spirit so that He can work through us. As followers of Jesus, we come to understand that not owning ourselves is actually a good thing!

When we get out of the way and understand ourselves as stewards of our bodies and entire lives – rather than owners and definers of the self – we understand that our responsibility is so much greater than just to ourselves. *We are responsible for everything that God has given us and put around us because it is all His even as we are entirely His.* The best part is that when we are fully surrendered to Him, The Holy Spirit inside us makes us capable of far more than we could ever accomplish on our own — all for the glory of His Kingdom.

Ask yourself these questions:

What aspects of life do I like to be in control of and/or independent in? How is God inviting me to be more dependent on Him? How is the Lord inviting me to steward myself and my resources for the benefit of His Kingdom?

Pray this prayer:

Lord, forgive me for my own attempts to define myself and find my own way. I surrender to Your definition of me and to my role as a steward of Your Kingdom. Help me to be faithful with the life that You have given me. Help me to fulfill my part of the Great Commission by Your Holy Spirit. I am not my own, Lord. I am Yours! I ask this in the name of the Father, and of the Son, and of the Holy Spirit. Amen.

As You Go, Making Disciples #4

by Deryk Richenburg

"I am a steward. My mission as a disciple of Jesus Christ is to make more and better disciples for Him everywhere I go. It is the outworking of my loving devotion to Christ and His Church."

I appeal to you for my child, Onesimus, whose father I became in my imprisonment. (Philemon 1:10)

When Paul wrote to Philemon, he was confined in prison. Many of us have never experienced imprisonment. However, after the Covid-19 pandemic, we understand confinement quite well. We know what it is like to self-quarantine. We understand the emotions and thoughts that accompany it.

During our Covid-19 confinement, we might have begun to believe that God's work and, subsequently, our work of making disciples was confined as well. However, Paul's imprisonment along with meeting Onesimus shifts that mindset.

God moved in mighty ways in bringing Onesimus to Paul. Onesimus was a bondservant who ran away from Paul's friend Philemon. He fled to Rome. Somehow, in some way that only God could orchestrate, he visited Paul in prison. Those visits with Paul changed Onesimus' life forever.

Paul responded to God's introduction by doing what he always did. He made disciples wherever he went. Paul wrote in the passage above that he became Onesimus' father. Paul uses a word to describe the father's role in producing offspring. Paul uses this word in describing his relationship with the Corinthian church (1 Corinthians 4:15) as well as the Galatian church (Galatians 4:19). Paul is saying that he became the spiritual father to Onesimus. *He discipled him while he was in prison.*

Like Paul, we are called to disciple others wherever we go. We are to do it at church, in confinement, in our families and at work. Making disciples is *a lifestyle that follows us wherever we are—even in prison.*

Ask yourself these questions:

What are the mighty ways that God is working in my life to lead others to Him? Am I praying for them? Am I discipling them so that they might know and look like Jesus?

Pray this prayer:

Lord, I pray that you would help me to see the people around me that you want me to disciple. Give me courage to build relationships with them. Give me boldness to pray for them. Give me insight so that I might help them draw closer to You. In Jesus' name. Amen.

As You Go, Making Disciples #5

by John Kimball

"I am a steward. My mission as a disciple of Jesus Christ is to make more and better disciples for Him everywhere I go. It is the outworking of my loving devotion to Christ and His Church."

> *... and what you have heard from me in the presence of many witnesses entrust to faithful men, who will be able to teach others also. (2 Timothy 2:2)*

Disciples make disciples. It sounds so simple, and yet so many today either refuse to do it or are ignorant of this fact. Many churches don't make it an expectation. But Jesus' commission to us deputizes us to make disciples. It's what disciples do. I still remember the day I was challenged by an older pastor about the lack of disciple making in my church at the time. He said, "Look, if they aren't making disciples, then they are not yet disciples of Jesus themselves because that's what real disciples do!"

As Paul writes to his son-in-the-faith, Timothy, he expresses just how prolific this disciple making is to be for us. He shows that disciple making is a generational enterprise – going at least four spiritual generations deep. Paul (first generation) has discipled Timothy (second generation). Timothy is to entrust that same discipleship into the lives of reliable men (third generation), and they will in turn teach others also (fourth generation). In my own heart, I've come to believe that discipleship is not truly what it is meant to be unless it is occurring spiritual generation to spiritual generation, one after the other.

The conviction I felt that day changed my ministry. It took me a long time to develop such generational fruit, but it did happen. I began almost immediately by choosing a handful of leaders, teaching them to follow my example. I will never forget the excitement we all felt the day one of those men began investing in a disciple of his own. Disciples make disciples. They grow into it, but it is a non-negotiable.

Ask yourself these questions:

Am I making disciples for Jesus? If I am not making disciples, what does that say about my own relationship with my Savior as a disciple? If I were to begin investing in someone today, who would it be? How will I invite them?

Pray this prayer:

Father, show me how to make more and better disciples of Jesus. Connect me with the people and the resources I need to do this in a way that bears the most fruit for Your kingdom and glory. Help me to start a generational disciple-making cycle that continues well after I am at home with You. Amen.

As You Go, Making Disciples #6

by Dr. Tom Johnston

"I will be a witness who shares with others the comfort that I myself have received from God through Jesus Christ."

Blessed be the God and Father of our Lord Jesus Christ, the Father of mercies and God of all comfort, who comforts us in all our affliction, so that we may be able to comfort those who are in any affliction, with the comfort with which we ourselves are comforted by God. For as we share abundantly in Christ's sufferings, so through Christ we share abundantly in comfort too. If we are afflicted, it is for your comfort and salvation; and if we are comforted, it is for your comfort, which you experience when you patiently endure the same sufferings that we suffer. (2 Corinthians 1:3–6)

I've noticed that when the Lord walks someone through a difficult situation in their life, within six months He is using that person to minister His love and comfort to others who are going through a similar circumstance. Our pain is not wasted by God – He uses the story of how we He got us through it to bless others. The comfort we receive is the comfort we give.

In John 9 there is an amazing story of how Jesus heals a man born blind. The guy never actually sees Jesus – he was blind after all! He doesn't know where Jesus is, doesn't have the right theology concerning who He is, and yet considers himself to be a disciple of Christ. When the Pharisees mocked him, saying Jesus was a sinner, the guy's reply was amazing:

He answered, 'Whether he is a sinner I do not know. One thing I do know, that though I was blind, now I see.' (John 9:25)

At this point, he had not yet seen Jesus, didn't know where He was, and had some incomplete theology – *but he knew what had happened to him.* He knew what Jesus had done. His personal story of healing and transformation was what he had to share.

So, you probably have never seen Jesus, you don't know where He is (unless you have a multi-dimensional GPS locked on heaven!), and your theology is imperfect. But you do know your story, you do know what Jesus has done in your life – and you can share that with others for their comfort. So, share your Jesus story! Look for those who are going through things which Jesus has already walked you through. Be His love in action – *give away the comfort you have received!*

Ask yourself these questions:

What is my story of God's comfort? Who do I need to share God's comfort with?

Pray this prayer:

Father God, thank You for walking me through all the difficult seasons and situations in my life. Help me to understand my story so I can share it with others. Holy Spirit, please direct me to those whom I can comfort with my story of God's love and grace in my life. I pray this in the name of the Father, and of the Son, and of the Holy Spirit. Amen.

As You Go, Making Disciples #7

by Tim McGinnin Jr.

"I will be a witness who shares with others the comfort that I myself have received from God through Jesus Christ."

One thing I do know, that though I was blind, now I see. (John 9:25b)

John 9 captures the testimony of a man born blind who was forever changed after a brief encounter with Jesus. We don't know the man's name, but his story is one that created an enormous amount of commotion in his time and is one that encourages and awes followers of Christ to this day. It even inspired a line in John Newton's famous hymn, Amazing Grace. This man spent his days waiting for others to give him money and food so he could survive. All that changed after a brief encounter with the Messiah who "anointed the man's eyes with mud" after spitting in the dirt (John 9:6-7). After washing the mud away as instructed by Jesus, the man could see for the first time in his life. It was indeed a miracle! Not only was he physically changed, but this encounter resulted in the man becoming a disciple of Jesus, also changing his eternal destiny (v. 27, 38). This brought about many questions, especially from the religious leaders of the day.

The man and his family were interrogated about his history and the legitimacy of his claims of being healed by Jesus. They tried to convince him that there was no way that Jesus could have done such a thing. He did not have all of the right answers about who Jesus was and what He was up to. The man had only just met Jesus for the first time after all. *But one thing he was absolutely convinced of was what Christ had done for him in that powerful moment of healing.* In those moments, and undoubtedly in many others throughout the rest of that man's life, he witnessed to others about the comfort and healing of God that he experienced through Jesus.

Wherever we find ourselves in our journey with Christ, we are called to share the story of what the Lord has done in and through us with others. We do not need to have all the answers to the difficult questions that people wrestle with. We will grow in our knowledge and understanding of the Lord over time as we pursue Him, but we never fully figure it all out on this side of eternity. Yet we can be convinced of what Jesus has done in and through our lives and we can be faithful to share our story with others as we go throughout our lives.

Ask yourself these questions:

What has the Lord done for me (what has He freed me from, healed, restored, and so on?) that I need to share with others? Who are the people who know me who have seen changes in my life as a result of knowing Jesus? How is the Lord inviting me to be a witness to people in my circles of relationship right now?

Pray this prayer:

Lord, help me to be confident in the testimony of who You are and what You've done in my life. Help me to be a bold witness to the people in my life. God, use me to bring others into relationship with you! I pray this in the name of the Father, and of the Son, and of the Holy Spirit. Amen.

As You Go, Making Disciples #8

by John Kimball

"I will be a witness who shares with others the comfort that I myself have received from God through Jesus Christ."

Blessed be the God and Father of our Lord Jesus Christ, the Father of mercies and God of all comfort, who comforts us in all our affliction, so that we may be able to comfort those who are in any affliction, with the comfort with which we ourselves are comforted by God. For as we share abundantly in Christ's sufferings, so through Christ we share abundantly in comfort too. (2 Corinthians 1:3-5)

Everyone has a story. Mine has hills and valleys – some mountains, and some really deep gorges. There were three seasons in my life when I clung to the God of all Comfort.

The year I graduated college; I experienced a very deep depression. I was suicidal. I traversed this horrible journey without Jesus. It was awful. However, the circumstances surrounding this depression ultimately drove me to Christ.

Near the end of my first pastorate, my dad died. He was an ox of a man. He loved Jesus. He ministered by my side on 15 global missionary trips. We were like glue. I had lost people before, but the depth of my grief was insurmountable. It took a long time to process through that loss.

As I began my most recent church planting adventure, I had some serious health issues that so traumatized my body and mind that I endured severe clinical anxiety and panic attacks for over two years. Medication and counseling helped, but it was Jesus who embraced me through it.

In each of these cases, *the Father opened before me significant doors of ministry I could not have known without the pain.* I have spoken to many suicidal people over the years – they could not believe I actually understood their pain. I have walked with grieving family members in some really tragic situations. I could comfort them because I had been in the same anguish. And I'm amazed at how many people – in person and even on social media – have responded to my openness about my anxiety. It has boggled my mind how our paths continue to "coincidentally" cross. I can comfort them with the comfort I, myself, have received. And some of these have turned to Christ as a result. Our God never wastes any experience.

Ask yourself these questions:

How have I received comfort in my own times of pain or desperation? How has God led me through that experience, and what did I learn that can help others? How can I bring service out of my pain, to help others who are enduring similar circumstances?

Pray this prayer:

Father, show me how I can use my own comfort to comfort others. Then, would You please bring such people across my daily path? Thank you. Amen.

As You Go, Making Disciples #9

by Tim McGinnin Jr.

"I will be a witness who shares with others the comfort that I myself have received from God through Jesus Christ."

> *But you will receive power when the Holy Spirit has come upon you, and you will be my witnesses in Jerusalem and in all Judea and Samaria, and to the end of the earth. (Acts 1:8)*

There is an order of events in this passage of Scripture that could be easy to miss if we read it too quickly. The first thing Jesus tells his disciples is that they will receive power when the Holy Spirit comes upon them, which is what's about to happen on Pentecost in Acts 2 if you read a little further ahead. He then says from that point of empowerment in the Holy Spirit, they will be His witnesses, first right where they are and ultimately expanding to the ends of the earth. When we read through the rest of the book of Acts in the Bible, we see witnessing in the empowerment of the Holy Spirit play out throughout the entire narrative of the early church.

Generally speaking, a witness is a person who gives testimony or evidence about something that has happened to them, that they know to be true, or that they have seen take place. In a legal situation, witnesses are used in court to verify the facts about events and various circumstances of whatever is under scrutiny by the court. As witnesses of Jesus Christ, our testimony concerns the evidence for the activity of the Holy Spirit in and through us. And it is by that very empowerment of the Lord dwelling in us through the Holy Spirit that we are even able to share that evidence with others! We do not witness in our own strength and with our own words. We do so under the power and unction of the Holy Spirit.

When we find ourselves in the most difficult circumstances, the

Holy Spirit gives us the words to say (Matthew 10:19). Stephen, the first martyr of the faith, was said to be "full of grace and power" and "doing great wonders and signs among the people" (Acts 6:8) right before he was seized, tried, preached before the Jewish high council, and stoned to death. Stephen was witnessing in the power of the Holy Spirit right up until his life ended. Interestingly enough, the word *martyr* that we use to describe someone who dies for their faith in Christ, comes from the Greek word that means "witness." The majority of Christians in the Western world today will not be martyrs who die for their faith; however, we are all called to be witnesses of Jesus Christ through the power of the Holy Spirit for our entire lives.

Ask yourself this question:

How is the Lord inviting me to witness to others today?

Pray this prayer:

Lord, empower me afresh by Your Holy Spirit so that I might be Your witness for Your glory! Help me to be bold in Your Spirit so that I might boldly proclaim Your Gospel so that others might come to know You. Give me the words to say in opportunities You provide for me to be Your witness. Help me to see what it is You are doing and to partner with that alone. I pray this in the name of the Father, and of the Son, and of the Holy Spirit. Amen.

As You Go, Making Disciples #10

by Marjorie Clark

"I will be a witness who shares with others the comfort that I myself have received from God through Jesus Christ."

Blessed be the God and Father of our Lord Jesus Christ, the Father of mercies and God of all comfort, who comforts us in all our affliction, so that we may be able to comfort those who are in any affliction, with the comfort with which we ourselves are comforted by God. For as we share abundantly in Christ's sufferings, so through Christ we share abundantly in comfort too. (2 Corinthians 1:3-4)

I am seeing something in Paul's words that I never considered until now. He blesses the God and Father of our Lord Jesus Christ, who is the Father of mercies and God of all comfort. Therefore, I conclude that He comforted Jesus in His sufferings ... and He abundantly comforted His Son – or we would not be the recipients of Christ's abundant comfort. The Father of mercies – mercies which put Jesus on Calvary for our salvation – is also the God of ALL comfort. I don't think I've ever considered the Father's loving comfort of Jesus, in Gethsemane, in front of the Jewish council, in the presence of the soldiers who beat Him, and then crucified Him. If God the Father comforts us in ALL our afflictions, then He also comforted Jesus. Until. Until that moment when He had to look away as Jesus became our sin-bearer. "My God, my God, why have you forsaken me?" In great affliction, we can feel like God has turned His back on us. But that will never happen to you or to me ... because it happened to Jesus. I don't understand it. But that's not the point. I simply need to remember it. When I don't have answers. When it appears that God isn't present, doesn't care about my pain... I need to remember Who He is, and what He has done because of His great love for me. I need to remember that He promised to never leave me or forsake me.

He comforts us, not by answering our 'why', but *by being present in mercy and love*. Therefore, we are fully able to comfort those who are in ANY affliction with that same comfort. We don't need to have experienced the same 'affliction' – we only need to have been comforted by our God and Father. We don't bring answers, or 'fixes', or 'religion' because they don't heal the heart's wounds. We bring presence, love, and comfort. So, the question is, have you been comforted by God? If so, that's what you need to share.

Ask yourself this question:

When and how have I received God's comfort? How can I share that comfort with someone today?

Pray this prayer:

Father, I am forever thankful that you are both the Father of mercies and the God of all comfort. I live in a world where people are hurting. Many are afflicted with sorrow, depression, and loss. Help me share with them the comfort You have shown me. I need greater understanding of Your comforting ways. Show me what to say and what not to say. Teach me to pray first and continually for those You lead me to share Your comfort with. Make me a true witness of the mercy and comfort You have shown me. I pray this in the name of Your Son, my Lord Jesus Christ. Amen.

As You Go, Making Disciples #11

by Dr. Tom Johnston

"Making disciples is my third priority."

And Jesus came and said to them, "All authority in heaven and on earth has been given to me. Go therefore and make disciples of all nations, baptizing them in the name of the Father and of the Son and of the Holy Spirit, teaching them to observe all that I have commanded you. And behold, I am with you always, to the end of the age." (Matthew 28:18-20)

The Great Commandments of Matthew 22:34-40 tell us to love God with everything we are and to love and serve others as we would ourselves. The Great Commission tells us to share with others how that happens. If loving God and loving others are our first and second priorities in life, making disciples is our third. These three priorities combine to direct our lives in the way of Jesus. Even as we create space and time for developing our relationship with the Lord, and even as we invest similarly in loving and caring for others, we must also allow disciple-making to make demands on us. Devotion to Christ leads to devotion to His Church and His mission.

It is His intention that His disciples (us) make more disciples. It is not something left to the "professionals," the pastors and other leaders. It is something for all of us to invest in - *our time, talent and treasure*. His mission should be a priority which supersedes our own wants and desires. We shouldn't waste our time on useless things – the Lord owns our time. We need to spend it on people who are seeking to follow Jesus. Our talents and spiritual gifts should not be wasted or left unused – they should be invested in the Kingdom work. We don't need more, newer, bigger, better of anything – we need to use our financial resources to further the mission. Christ gave us a *directive* to make disciples, not a *suggestion* that we should. Our engagement in mission is a natural outflow of our love for Him and others, and as such, becomes a priority of our life.

Ask yourself these questions:

Is disciple-making a priority for me in time, talent and treasure? Who is discipling me? Who am I discipling?

Pray this prayer:

Father God, thank you for calling me as a disciple of Jesus and His way. Holy Spirit, I ask You to prompt me continually to have disciple-making as my third priority. Show me how to intentionally engage in making disciples with those around me. I pray this in the name of the Father, and of the Son, and of the Holy Spirit. Amen.

As You Go, Making Disciples #12

by Dr. Tom Johnston

"Making disciples is my third priority."

> *"Look carefully then how you walk, not as unwise but as wise, making the best use of the time, because the days are evil." (Ephesians 5:15-16)*

The days we live in are indeed evil, perhaps more so than any other in our generation. Our response to such a situation is not to run and hide in fear, but engage all the more aggressively in Kingdom extension. The Kingdom advances one heart at a time, so the antidote for evil is to see more people become disciples of Jesus. In this passage, the Apostle Paul is telling them to literally "buy back the time," to pay the price for the Kairos moment – the specially appointed time – they find themselves in.

Like the Ephesians, we find ourselves in days filled with evil, yet it is a season of opportunity for the Gospel to spread. We need to invest our time in a sacrificial fashion in disciple-making. Rather than sit around complaining about the state of affairs we find ourselves in, we must devote our time to the advancement of the Kingdom. People right around us are ready to take their next steps forward with Christ. Some may not even know Him yet. Still, the Holy Spirit has been at work. Truly, He is just waiting for us to make ourselves available to Him and those whom he is working in. This will cost us our *time.*

We must buy back the time from those things which are worthless, that bear no fruit in the Kingdom mission of Jesus. Instead of spending our time on social media, we could instead pray for those the Lord is laying on our hearts. Rather than video gaming for hours on end, we could give that time to those wanting to know more about Jesus. In place of a Netflix binge, why not use that time to help someone develop their relationship with the

Lord? We are all busy people, and recreation is an important use of our time. But how can we "buy back" the time that we waste?

We need to open time in our calendar to build relationships that facilitate others coming to know Christ, and for others, growing in their relationship with Him. We need to open our homes, our living rooms, our dinner table, all with the focus on investing in the eternal future of those seeking to follow Christ. In redeeming the time of these evil days, we can join Christ in His mission of making disciples – *which is our third priority.*

Ask yourself these questions:

What time am I wasting that I can "buy back" for the Kingdom? Who can I invest my time in to see them become a disciple of Jesus?

Pray this prayer:

Father God, thank you for gift of time. Holy Spirit, I ask that You show me how to invest my time in disciple-making. Open my eyes to the ways that I waste time, so that I might buy it back for the Kingdom. I pray this in the name of the Father, and of the Son, and of the Holy Spirit. Amen.

As You Go, Making Disciples #13

by Dr. Tom Johnston

"Making disciples is my third priority."

> *Now there are varieties of gifts, but the same Spirit; and there are varieties of service, but the same Lord; and there are varieties of activities, but it is the same God who empowers them all in everyone. To each is given the manifestation of the Spirit for the common good. (1 Corinthians 12:4–7)*

It is truly amazing how God has shaped each one of us! As the Scripture says:

> *For you formed my inward parts; you knitted me together in my mother's womb. I praise you, for I am fearfully and wonderfully made. (Psalm 139:13-14a)*

As we grew inside our mothers, He was already at work shaping us, preparing us to serve Him. Our mental and physical abilities were being formed for His future purposes. Yet, His work was not finished in the womb, but His shaping has continued throughout our lives:

> *And we know that for those who love God all things work together for good, for those who are called according to his purpose. (Romans 8:28)*

God has been using, and continues to use, everything in our life – *the good and the bad* – to shape us to fulfill His purposes. Every experience has shaped us. Our intellectual, education and physical development has been guided by the Lord – all for His Kingdom purposes. Our natural talents, skills and abilities, along with the Gifts of the Holy Spirit, all combine into a package of "grace empowerment," preparing us for His service:

> *For we are his workmanship, created in Christ Jesus for good works, which God prepared beforehand, that we should walk in them. (Ephesians 2:10)*

Even as we are His masterpiece, the work of His hands, we are ourselves being shaped to make a contribution to His Kingdom work. We come to know what that work is when we press into our relationship with Him:

> *I cry out to God Most High, to God who fulfills his purpose for me. (Psalm 57:2)*

As our third priority is to participate with Jesus in making more and better disciples for Him, we need to employ all of our grace empowerment towards this goal. Far too often people neglect their gifts and don't use them, or spend their skills and abilities on things other than the Kingdom work. We need to prioritize the use of our talents, abilities and spiritual gifts for the purposes for which the Father created us. Don't waste them – use them for the eternal benefit of others!

Ask yourself these questions:

How am I using my "grace empowerment" to make disciples? Is disciple-making a priority for me?

Pray this prayer:

Father God, thank You for making me as You have – with the talents, abilities and spiritual gifts You have placed within me. Holy Spirit, I ask that You guide me in the use of my grace empowerment, directing me to use what I have to become a stronger disciple of Christ. I pray this in the name of the Father, and of the Son, and of the Holy Spirit. Amen.

As You Go, Making Disciples #14

by Tim McGinnin Jr.

"Making disciples is my third priority."

> *And Jesus came and said to them, "All authority in heaven and on earth has been given to me. Go therefore and make disciples of all nations, baptizing them in the name of the Father and of the Son and of the Holy Spirit, teaching them to observe all that I have commanded you. And behold, I am with you always, to the end of the age." (Matthew 28:18-20)*

When we embrace our identities as children of God, we have a deeper appreciation and understanding of who He is as our Father. When we understand ourselves as servants, we have a deeper understanding and appreciation of Christ as the ultimate servant who provided the example of sacrificial service for us. And when we understand our roles as stewards, living a fully surrendered life that is not our own, we understand and appreciate more deeply who God is as Lord, Master, and King. Embracing and growing into our identities as sons and daughters, our capacities as servants, and destinies as stewards is all part of the journey of walking with the Lord in this life. As we know and understand Him more, we know and understand ourselves more, too.

The order of the three priorities of Loving God, Loving Others, and Making Disciples is incredibly important, and they are all completely necessary for a Christian to live a life unto the Lord. You can't eliminate any of the priorities. You cannot re-order them either. They build on each other. We can only effectively make disciples as we go throughout our lives if we love God first with everything we are even as we are loved by Him with everything He is, and if we love others in the same way that Jesus loves us. In the Great Commission (Matthew 28:18-20 above), Jesus tells

His disciples (and us) that they are to teach the disciples they make to observe all that He commanded them—which is loving God and loving others (Matthew 22:34-40). If we don't have a solid foundation of loving God and loving others, then what are we actually teaching other people to do? We can't give away what we don't have. *Making disciples is not a lower priority because it comes in as the third priority*. It's simply impossible to make disciples of Jesus *if we don't have foundations of the first two priorities in our lives* to give away in our discipleship of others. Let's love God radically and extravagantly, love others with the self-sacrificing love of Christ, and out of that teach those around us to do the same.

Ask yourself these questions:

How am I being intentional about developing the three priorities of the Irreducible Core in my own life? What have I learned about loving God and loving others that I can teach others in discipleship? Who is the Lord calling me to intentionally disciple?

Pray this prayer:

Lord, help me to know You more deeply as my Father so I understand who I am as Your child. Help me understand Your sacrifice more deeply so I can go and serve others with Your love. Help me to fully embrace You as my Lord and my King so that I can live a life of faithful stewardship for You, making disciples everywhere I go, advancing the Kingdom of God. I pray this in the name of the Father, and of the Son, and of the Holy Spirit. Amen.

As You Go, Making Disciples #15

by Dr. Tom Johnston

"Making disciples is my third priority."

One who is faithful in a very little is also faithful in much, and one who is dishonest in a very little is also dishonest in much. If then you have not been faithful in the unrighteous wealth, who will entrust to you the true riches? And if you have not been faithful in that which is another's, who will give you that which is your own? No servant can serve two masters, for either he will hate the one and love the other, or he will be devoted to the one and despise the other. You cannot serve God and money. (Luke 16:10-13)

In Luke 16:1-13, Jesus told the parable of the Dishonest Manager, who was caught skimming from his master's finances. The man in the story was the financial agent for his lord. Jesus never addressed the white-collar crime in this tale, but rather focused on the shrewd adaptation the manager made when caught. The deals he cut with those who owed his master money were designed to secure a future position with one of them when he was finally terminated by his lord.

The purpose of this story is to show us how we should use the financial resources entrusted to us: they are to be used for the work of the Kingdom, and not just spent on the things of this life. When we do this, we will ensure that we have many friends awaiting us in heaven! We must use our funds shrewdly, figuring how to adapt our lives to allow for more of our finances to be freed up for Kingdom work.

Jesus highlighted three other important elements when explaining this parable. First, that those who are faithful to use the financial resources entrusted to them for the Kingdom work, will have yet *more* financial resources released to them for even *greater* Kingdom impact:

> *And God is able to make all grace abound to you, so that having all sufficiency in all things at all times, you may abound in every good work. As it is written, 'He has distributed freely, he has given to the poor; his righteousness endures forever.' He who supplies seed to the sower and bread for food will supply and multiply your seed for sowing and increase the harvest of your righteousness. (2 Corinthians 9:7-10)*

The second point Jesus made was that the use of financial resources is simply a set of "training wheels" for the true riches of spiritual gifts. Natural resources used well and in accordance with His will shows how we will use the Gifts of the Holy Spirit.

The third point He made is that of *paradigm*: you cannot use financial resources according to the pattern of the world *and* the needs of the Kingdom. It's not a "both/and," but rather an "either/or." A choice is required – in regards to the use of finances, which "master" will we serve? The world or the Kingdom?

Disciple-making, as our third priority, has a claim on our finances, as it is the Kingdom purpose of the Church. Local and global mission are both funded by the resources the Lord has entrusted to us. May we use them shrewdly, making many friends who will spend eternity with us!

Ask yourself these questions:

Am I "skimming" from My Master's finances which have been entrusted to me? Am I using what I have been given according to His Kingdom purposes?

Pray this prayer:

Father God, thank You for providing all my needs – and the ability to partner with You in financing Your Kingdom work. Holy Spirit,

I ask that You lead me in my financial investment in the ministry of the Kingdom. Show me how to intentionally use the funds entrusted to me in making disciples. I pray this in the name of the Father, and of the Son, and of the Holy Spirit. Amen.

SPIRITUAL DISCIPLINES

In pursuit of this I will give myself to the practice of spiritual disciplines

"I submit my life to The Holy Scriptures - The Word of God."

"I will practice daily the presence of the Holy Spirit through reflective prayer."

"I will depend on the empowering presence of the Holy Spirit in my life and ministry."

"I am devoted to The Fellowship—living a shared life together in Christ as family and community."

"I am devoted to The Breaking of Bread—the celebration of the Lord's Supper and the practice of hospitality."

"I will practice generosity through tithing as a means of personal discipline, giving offerings as an act of love and providing for the needs of others."

"I will lovingly, gently and graciously share with others the story

of how God's love and grace has transformed my heart and life."

Spiritual Disciplines #1

by Dr. Tom Johnston

"I submit my life to The Holy Scriptures - The Word of God."

> *And they devoted themselves to the apostles' teaching and fellowship, to the breaking of bread and the prayers. (Acts 2:42)*

When we read about the early Church – the first Christians, we see several things that are a hallmark of the Christian faith. One of the most central of these is the Scripture. Why? Because through the Scripture, the Bible, we can come to know who God is, understand His heart of love for us and learn how to have a relationship with Him. People coming into a relationship with God through His one and only begotten Son, Jesus Christ, is what Christianity is all about, and the Bible is key to this happening.

The Scripture covers about 3,000 years of human history, and is the second most significant way God has revealed Himself to us, with Jesus being the fullest, most complete revelation of who God is (John 14:6). Indeed, He Himself said that the Scripture pointed to Him (John 5:39). It is the "way," the path of what following Jesus looks like. Through the Bible, the Holy Spirit teaches us, corrects us and trains us In His way:

> *All Scripture is breathed out by God and profitable for teaching, for reproof, for correction, and for training in righteousness, that the man of God may be complete, equipped for every good work. (2 Timothy 3:16-17)*

The Bible tells us about the nature of God and how He has dealt with people throughout history. It explains the plan God has for re-establishing our relationship with Him. Scripture details the covenant relationship we have with God through Jesus, and the rights and responsibilities, the promises and expectations which are part of that relationship. It speaks to us of things of eternity and very practical things about living everyday life. Through it, and the working of the Holy Spirit in us, we can grow and mature as people, and as followers of Christ, becoming conformed to His image. Because of this, the Christian disciple must develop a daily discipline of reading the Scripture, even just a chapter a day can begin to make a huge difference.

Ask yourself this question:

How can I order my life around the daily reading of the Scripture?

Pray this prayer:

My Father in heaven, thank You for giving me the Bible. I ask that Your Holy Spirit open my heart and mind to understand what You have written. Help me to not only know it, but to live it as well, in and through every aspect of my life. May it be so, I ask in the name of the Father, and of the Son, and of the Holy Spirit. Amen.

Spiritual Disciplines #2

by Dr. Tom Johnston

"I submit my life to The Holy Scriptures - The Word of God."

> *Behold, the days are coming, declares the LORD, when I will make a new covenant with the house of Israel and the house of Judah, not like the covenant that I made with their fathers on the day when I took them by the hand to bring them out of the land of Egypt, my covenant that they broke, though I was their husband, declares the LORD. For this is the covenant that I will make with the house of Israel after those days, declares the LORD: I will put my law within them, and I will write it on their hearts. And I will be their God, and they shall be my people. And no longer shall each one teach his neighbor and each his brother, saying, 'Know the LORD,' for they shall all know me, from the least of them to the greatest, declares the LORD. For I will forgive their iniquity, and I will remember their sin no more. (Jeremiah 31:31-34)*

Everything about humanity's relationship with our Creator is about our covenant with Him. A covenant is an agreement between two parties, with both sides having rights and responsibilities. The Bible itself is divided into Old and New Covenants, the story of God's redemptive work being embodied in a covenant relationship with Israel in the Old Testament, and with the Church in the New Testament. The Bible contains the covenant expectations of God for His people, as well as the covenant benefits His people enjoy through their covenant with Him. Knowing the Scripture helps us understand what the Lord expects from us in our relationship with Him (and others) and what we can expect from Him as our Heavenly Father.

Jesus said "If you love me, you will keep my commandments" (John 14:15), so the way we express our love for the Lord is to obediently follow His will for us. Having the Bible is such a privilege for us, as we can know His heart and mind on any subject of life. We are able to live in accordance with the loving covenant we have through Jesus. As we submit the way we live our everyday lives to the guidance of the Holy Spirit through the Scriptures we can keep covenant with God – who has always, and will always keep His covenant with us!

Ask yourself these questions:

Do I understand what God expects from me as a child of God? DO I understand the blessing that I have as part of the Father's covenant with me has His child?

Pray this prayer:

Father God, thank You for the revelation of Your will through Your Word. Holy Spirit, guide me through the Scriptures, and lead me through them each and every day as I walk in covenant with my Father. I pray this in the name of the Father, and of the Son, and of the Holy Spirit. Amen.

Spiritual Disciplines #3

by Dr. Tom Johnston

"I submit my life to The Holy Scriptures - The Word of God."

> *I will run in the way of your commandments when you enlarge my heart! Teach me, O LORD, the way of your statutes; and I will keep it to the end. Give me understanding, that I may keep your law and observe it with my whole heart. Lead me in the path of your commandments, for I delight in it. (Psalm 119:32-35)*

In the Old Testament, the word for "law" is Torah, and means instruction, direction in the way. In our culture, the word law has a different meaning, usually understood as "rules." God's word, His law as embodied in the Scriptures has always been about helping humanity know how to walk in the way that God has intended for us, walking in loving obedience with our Creator. As we learn His word, we learn His way:

> *With my whole heart I seek you; let me not wander from your commandments! I have stored up your word in my heart, that I might not sin against you. (Psalm 119:10-11)*

Ultimately, all the Scriptures point to Jesus Christ, who is *"the way, and the truth, and the life"* (John 14:6), as He said:

> *You search the Scriptures because you think that in them you have eternal life; and it is they that bear witness about me. (John 5:39)*

Jesus Himself is the ultimate embodiment of the Father's will, and the perfect example of the Father's *torah*, or way, lived out. The more we submit ourselves to His Word, the more we know Him and His way. In all of this, the Holy Spirit, who is Christ in us, can empower us to live the way of Jesus in our lives every day:

> *"If you love me, you will keep my commandments. And I will ask the Father, and he will give you another Helper, to be with you forever, even the Spirit of truth, whom the world cannot receive, because it neither sees him nor knows him. You know him, for he dwells with you and will be in you. (John 14:15-17)*

As we submit how we live out our daily lives to the word of God, the Scriptures, we can expect the Holy Spirit to empower us to live them. Trust and expect the Holy Spirit to lead you into all truth, and to help you build your life upon the Word of God!

Ask yourself these questions:

Am I submitted to the way of God as expressed in the Bible? Do I trust the Holy Spirit to guide and lead me through the Scriptures?

Pray this prayer:

Father God, I thank you for the revelation of Your way through Your Word. Holy Spirit, guide me to walk the way of Jesus as made known to me through the Scriptures. Help me to align my daily life with the revealed will of God that I can see and know through the Bible. I pray this in the name of the Father, and of the Son, and of the Holy Spirit. Amen.

Spiritual Disciplines #4

by Tim McGinnin Jr.

"I submit my life to The Holy Scriptures - The Word of God."

> *For the word of God is living and active, sharper than any two-edged sword, piercing to the division of soul and of spirit, of joints and of marrow, and discerning the thoughts and intentions of the heart. (Hebrews 4:12)*

The Bible is not a book we simply skim through or even read cover to cover once and thus attain some level of supreme spirituality or check it off a list of religious duties. I am not discounting the reading of Scripture from beginning to end as something we should do. In fact, as followers of Jesus, we should read through all of Scripture repeatedly throughout our lifetime. If there's anything we should read more than once in this life-it would be the Bible. We cannot treat the Bible like a normal book. We must approach it as the very Word of God for us today.

The writer of Hebrews said that the "word of God is living and active." I've found this to be so true in my own life. No matter how many times I've read Scripture, when I read it anew, listening to the Holy Spirit, He speaks to me through it and invites me to greater degrees of intimacy with Him and further obedience to His call on my life. There have been times when I've thought to myself "I don't want to read this again" or "I've read this plenty of times before" when I come to certain books or sections of Scripture. It is in those moments that I know in my flesh I am not approaching the Word as living and active. It is in those moments that I know I need to repent and posture myself properly to receive from the Lord through His Word. *When we spend time in the Word of God from a posture of submission and desire for connection to the Lord, the Word actually "reads" us in that very moment, and not only reveals God's heart to us but reveals our own hearts to ourselves as well.* The more I give myself to God through the reading and studying of Scripture, the more I get to know God and myself. The more He reveals Himself to me and the more He reveals my own heart to me, the more I can be an obedient son to my Father, the King of kings. The more I approach Scripture with the understanding that it is indeed living and active, the more I receive a life-giving deposit from the Lord—even the Scripture I've read so many times before and the things I may not naturally want to read in the moment.

As you sit to read the Word of God today, whether for the first time or the ten thousandth time, *expect* the Living Word to work *through* your discipline and speak to you for today.

Ask yourself these questions:

What are the barriers that I have encountered or am I currently encountering when it comes to spending consistent time reading Scripture? When was the last time I experienced the Word "reading me" as I read it? What did I learn from that time? What have I learned about God and myself through Scripture?

Pray this prayer:

Lord, thank You for the gift of Scripture that has preserved Your heart and Word for Your people for thousands of years! Help me to embrace the Word today and help me to be obedient to You through it. Reveal Yourself to me through the Word and show me my own heart through it as well. I ask in the name of the Father, and of the Son, and of the Holy Spirit. Amen.

Spiritual Disciplines #5

by Marjorie Clark

"I submit my life to The Holy Scriptures - The Word of God."

> *Your words were found, and I ate them, and your words became to me a joy and the delight of my heart, for I am called by your name, O LORD, God of hosts. (Jeremiah 15:16)*

As a young teen, I knew nothing of God or faith or Christianity except what I picked up in culture. Our family would occasionally go to church services on Easter, to please my father's sister. I had questions, but they were all internal as I lived under a "children should be seen but not heard" tradition. Somehow, at the wise age of eleven, I came across a Gideon Bible in my mother's bedroom and I discovered Psalm 23. I have no memory of how that happened, but everything I now know of God was planted as a small seed that evening as I sat and memorized that psalm "The Lord is my Shepherd, I shall not want ..."

Such is the power of the Word of God. Everything I love about God is spoken someplace in that psalm. His Word led me to the Shepherd and assured me of His love, provision, protection, presence, power ... and so much more. His Word drew me in, fed me, guided me, and cared for me. At any time in my now seven decades of life when I would wander off course, when I would be in danger, wounded, or lost, His Word would *speak* to me and *heal* me, *restore* me, *cleanse*, and *redirect* me.

My days now are bookmarked with the Word of God, from the first thing in the morning to the last thing at night. His presence always accompanies His Word and I hunger for it exceedingly. Have there been dry places? Yes – but only as I have ceased to seek Him first. When I've consumed other words, or been consumed by them, I have lost my taste for the purity of The Word.

But when I recognize my sin and confess it, He restores me with the fresh water of His Word and the fresh air of His Spirit – and I am revived. What about you? *What is your story as seen in relationship to His Word?*

Ask yourself these questions:

Do I truly hunger for the Word of God? If not, what is the reason? What one change can I make to increasingly seek the Lord in His Word?

Pray this prayer:

Jesus, I know You are my Good Shepherd but sometimes I feel like I'm just one among so, so many. I want to get closer to You. Thank You for calling me by Your name and for speaking to me in Your Word. I know Your Word is more than ink on paper, or an arrangement of vowels and consonants spoken from an app on my device. Your Word is powerful! Alive! Your Word is how I know You – and begin to know myself. Show me what may be keeping me from really meeting You in Your Word. I want to see breakthrough in my times in Your Word – I want to hunger for You and grow healthier and stronger in my faith walk. Holy Spirit, teach me Your ways, fill me, and lead me in Your paths. Speak to me. I'm listening. *(Pause for a few minutes and listen with a surrendered heart.)* ***Thank You for Your Living Word. Amen.***

Spiritual Disciplines #6

by Dr. Tom Johnston

"I will practice daily the presence of the Holy Spirit through reflective prayer."

> *My soul will be satisfied as with fat and rich food, and my mouth will praise you with joyful lips, when I remember you upon my bed, and meditate on you in the watches of the night; for you have been my help, and in the shadow of your wings I will sing for joy. My soul clings to you; your right hand upholds me. (Psalm 63:5-8)*

Reflection is the path to wisdom. Yet, often we say we are "too busy" to spend time thinking with God in prayer. And when we do pray, it tends to be a harried presentation of our "shopping list" for God. "Lord, I need this" or "Lord, I need you to do" that. While making our requests known to God is definitely part of prayer, the greater need is for us to listen. It's hard to hear someone when you are the one doing all the talking! The great reformer, Martin Luther is often quoted as saying he prayed two hours a day unless he was busy, then he would pray for three hours. SO, if you are going to be really busy in your day, better pray more!

Jesus went from one place of communion with the Father to another – *and in-between He did miracles.* He spent time alone with the Father (ref. Mark 1:35). He got away, He got alone with the Father – and He listened. He needed His marching orders so He could do what the Father was doing (ref. John 5:19). Brother Lawrence, a monk from the late Middle Ages, said that *"we should establish ourselves in a sense of God's Presence, by continually conversing with Him."* Ongoing reflection through such communion enables us to walk in a real-time "upload/download" in the Holy Spirit. The only limit to the "bandwidth" of this communication is how consistently we spend time thinking with

Him.

So, set yourself apart, dial back for several moments throughout your day. Set aside your agenda as you pray, focusing on listening. Praise Him, worship Him, read His Word – *then listen.* You will be surprised at how much more you become aware of the Holy Spirit moving throughout your day. You'll have less stress, less anxiety, less fear – *and more joy and energy!* Learn to practice the presence of God and reflect with Him in the Spirit.

Ask yourself these questions:

How much time do I spend reflecting in prayer? How can I adjust my day to do it more?

Pray this prayer:

Father God, teach me to practice Your presence daily. Holy Spirit, remind me to leave behind the craziness of my day and seek communion with the Father. Jesus, teach me Your path of reflection. I pray this in the name of the Father, and of the Son, and of the Holy Spirit. Amen.

Spiritual Disciplines #7

by Tim McGinnin Jr.

"I will practice daily the presence of the Holy Spirit through reflective prayer"

And he came to the disciples and found them sleeping. And he said to Peter, "So, could you not watch with me one hour? Watch and pray that you may not enter into temptation. The spirit indeed is willing, but the flesh is weak." (Matthew 26:40-41)

I remember a time early in my walk with the Lord when I felt convicted by the Holy Spirit to spend more time in prayer. Specifically, He was calling me to wake myself up early in the morning to devote more time to prayer. I'm a night-owl by nature so early mornings were never my favorite thing. But I could always pull it off if I was getting up to do something – so I figured this would work out no problem for a short season. Day 1, I woke up at 5:00am while it was still dark outside, hopped out of bed quietly so as not to disturb my sleeping wife and moved myself into the living room where I sat down in a chair and started to pray. I am not sure exactly how it happened but after what seemed to be about a minute or so went by, I found myself waking up again and more than an hour had actually passed! It was now time to get up and get ready for work —I slept through prayer. I wrestled through several more days of early wakeups and attempts to pray. Some days, I even forced myself to stand so that I wouldn't doze off. Some attempts were more successful than others and, in every situation, I felt the grogginess and exhaustion of waking up earlier than my body was used to. I'd like to say that eventually I pushed through and triumphantly engaged in powerful and passionate days of prayer but in this particular situation, I did not. I eventually gave up and felt like I failed. It wasn't long after that that I reread this passage in Matthew and realized that I had experienced the reality of Jesus' statement to His disciples when they fell asleep on Him in the Gethsemane: "The spirit indeed is willing, but the flesh is weak."

There will always be things that will push back on our need and even desires to daily engage the Lord through reflective prayer. Our own internal rhythms, the circumstances and seasons of life, and spiritual warfare are all things that get in the way and create barriers and inconsistencies in our prayer lives. That is, if we allow them to create barriers and inconsistencies. The other lesson I learned from that season of early morning prayer is that *I did not actually fail. I obediently woke myself up every morning and gave it what I had.* I was not satisfied with what I had to give because I wanted to have more endurance. I wanted that time to look a certain way and it did not. *But I was obedient*, and it did help me up my prayer game in general and *helped me to realize that my most focused time for prayer and other disciplines was early in the evening.* This helped to shape my regular rhythms and routines of prayer and discipline. There are still times though that I feel drawn to wake up earlier, or am awoken in the middle of the night, to pray. I may not always have the energy I wish I had to give in those moments, and while by body is feeling weak and tired, *my willing spirit can always win out* if I respond to the invitation of the Lord to engage Him in prayer with obedience.

Ask yourself these questions:

What is the best time of day for me to pray? How can I arrange my day so that prayer and time with the Lord in spiritual disciplines is prioritized? When was the last time I set up additional or special times of increased prayer and reflection with the Lord?

Pray this prayer:

Lord, help me to see where my flesh is weak when it comes to being intentional about spending time in prayer with You. Help me to see

the things that get in my way and help me to persevere through those things with obedience. God, thank You for Your grace and for accepting me even in weakness. Help me to embrace Your Holy Spirit in the midst of my weakness so that You might prove Yourself strong through me. I pray this in the name of the Father, and of the Son, and of the Holy Spirit. Amen.

Spiritual Disciplines #8

by Mike Chong Perkinson

"I will practice daily the presence of the Holy Spirit through reflective prayer."

Fear has a practice and love has a practice. The oddity of our lives is that no matter what we do, we are all disciplined to something or someone. We either practice fear or practice love. We become more proficient in what we practice.

It's been said that we are what we love. Maybe, more crassly and succinctly, we are what we want. Jesus stated it a bit differently in his 'mic drop' statement, "where your treasure is there your heart will be also." (Matthew 6:21)

Jesus' statement is profound in its simplicity as it tells us that our volitional capacity is completely surrendered to what we treasure. What that means in our day to day lives is that everyone is disciplined and committed to something or someone. For example, the person who is 25 minutes late is always 25 minutes late. *Their behavior is perfectly in line with their heart's treasure.*

Unless we admit and confess what our treasure is, change is impossible. No matter how hard one tries to change their behavior or will it to happen, it won't. The simple reason is that one's volition or will is already committed to a treasure.

The direction your life is going, what you are moving toward, reveals the treasure that your heart is embracing. We gravitate to the things we love and want and those things manifest in our time, energy, reflection, and money. *We all have a destination that we are moving toward that is housed in the Kingdom of God, the Kingdom of self, and/or the Kingdom of darkness.*

Ask yourself these questions:

Based on the direction of my life, what is my treasure? More simply,

who or what am I living for?
Is what I want or love what God wants and loves? Is it what He wants for me?
What do I need to surrender, repent of, and release to the Father today?

Pray this prayer:

Lord, "Search me, O God, and know my heart! Try me and know my thoughts! And see if there be any grievous way in me, and lead me in the way everlasting!" **(Psalms 139:23-24).** ***God, I give you all that I am today so that I might be who you created me to be in all that I say and do for your glory and delight. Amen.***

Spiritual Disciplines #9

by Selina McGinnin

"I will practice daily the presence of the Holy Spirit through reflective prayer."

For we are his workmanship, created in Christ Jesus for good works, which God prepared beforehand, that we should walk in them. (Ephesians 2:10)

Do you ever feel like you just don't know what you're doing or where you're going? In any given day there are plenty of distractions trying to get us to go a certain way and make certain choices. It's easy to get confused, overwhelmed, overstimulated, and busy. We know, because the Bible tells us, that we were created for a purpose and that good works were laid out for us before we were even born. If there is an actual design created for our lives to walk out and participate in, then shouldn't making decisions and figuring out what to do next be a little easier? Well, I suppose it would be if we changed up our focus and intentionality.

Let's look to Jesus as a prime example of living out the call that the Father had for Him. Jesus consistently and intentionally aligned Himself to the Father's will through reflective prayer. He got up early and went some place quiet to pray before His day started (Mark 1:35). He was quoted as saying He only did what He saw the Father doing (John 5:19). When the crowd wanted Him to stay, He spent time praying and learned the Father's plan was to continue to the next town. He left some place where everyone liked Him and was begging Him to stay because the Father said to continue on so the good news of the Kingdom could be preached (Luke 4:42-43). Sometimes we need to be willing to leave the comfortable for the good of the Kingdom. Those decisions can be tough but for Jesus, making decisions like that was easy because He was in regular, intentional, reflective prayer. In order to understand what God has for us and where He is leading us, we too must be intentional about the amount of time we are spending in reflective prayer.

Reflective prayer is a set apart time. A quiet time, where we listen and reflect on where we see God moving, what we know to the be the truth of His Word, and who God is. Reflective prayer is not just a laundry list of current prayer needs we recite in between errands where we are distracted by traffic, outside stimuli, or passengers in the car. Reflective prayer is an intentional listening and seeking of understanding so that you can be renewed by the Holy Spirit for the day's work and so that you can be prepared for where God is calling you.

It is possible to know where God is leading. It is possible to experience peace amid busyness and confusion. It is possible when we choose an intentional life that begins daily with quieting ourselves and our environment and entering into the presence of the Holy Spirit through reflective prayer.

Ask yourself these questions:

Am I fitting in quiet time with the Holy Spirit? Do busyness and distractions get in the way of taking time to listen to him? What is the biggest distraction?
Do I see what the Father is doing? Am I partnering with Him in it?

Pray this prayer:

Father, I'm tired of the unknown when I could know what You have for me if I only asked and spent time with You. Forgive me for putting the things of this life before You. God open up my ears to hear what You have to say and give me understanding and wisdom to walk out the call you have placed on my life. Holy Spirit, I invite you to lead me in all I do. Amen.

Spiritual Disciplines #10

by Marjorie Clark

"I will practice daily the presence of the Holy Spirit through reflective prayer."

> *Call to me and I will answer you, and will tell you great and hidden things that you have not known. (Jeremiah 33:3)*

The Holy Spirit is the one who brought us to life, who is our helper, our teacher, our comforter, and our reminder – the one who reminds us of everything Jesus said and did and continues to say and do in our lives. What an amazing gift!! He is not only our lifelong tutor who walks alongside us every step of the way, but He is the power of God resident within us to equip us to obey, to do our Father's will here on earth.

Can you imagine living with someone and *never having a conversation* with them? Perhaps you'd leave notes, lists of the things you'd like them to do. You might even shout out, as you walk out the door in the morning, "I love you! See you later." Sound ridiculous? It is unthinkable. Especially when that someone knows you better than you know yourself. Knows your every thought, your complete history, your hidden shame ... as well as your destiny and purpose and calling which are all birthed in the love of your Creator and Father and made possible for you in the sacrifice of His Only Begotten Son, our Lord Jesus, the Christ.

> *Search me, O God, and know my heart! Try me and know my thoughts! And see if there be any grievous way in me, and lead me in the way everlasting! (Psalm 139:23-24)*

The Holy Spirit is a communicator! He breathed the words of God to the writers of Scripture. It is He who brings those words to life and makes them powerful in your life. When I think of that, I just want to pour a cup of coffee and sit down and ask Him what He wants to say to me. What does He want me to know about myself? About today? About the people and activities that are on my heart?

If this discipline is new to you, or you simply aren't sure how to begin, here are some questions you can ask. When you do, pray from a place of vulnerability and honesty – you do not have to prove yourself to Him. He knows you and loves you.

Ask the Lord these questions:

Please show me the things I don't yet know...what I don't understand.
What is on Your heart today?
What is the answer to my prayer ...?
Please show me things I will need to know in order to walk the pathways You have for me.

Pray this prayer:

Father, thank you for the gift of Your Holy Spirit. Please forgive me for not being grateful, not recognizing Your goodness at work in my life. I want to know You and Your ways in my life. Keep reminding me to listen, to pay attention and to stay awake to what You are doing. I want to keep the conversation going. I love You and I want to love You with everything that is in me. I ask this in Your name, Father, and the name of Jesus, Your Son, and the name of Your Holy Spirit. Amen.

Spiritual Disciplines #11

by Dr. Tom Johnston

"I will depend on the empowering presence of the Holy Spirit in my life and ministry."

> *Abide in me, and I in you. As the branch cannot bear fruit by itself, unless it abides in the vine, neither can you, unless you abide in me. I am the vine; you are the branches. Whoever abides in me and I in him, he it is that bears much fruit, for apart from me you can do nothing. (John 15:4-5)*

Let's just admit it – without Jesus we'd all be in serious trouble! Without His life flowing into us and through us by the Holy Spirit, we would have nothing to bring to the table. Life would be an empty, continuous struggle, yet without victory. Our ministry efforts would be ineffective and frustrating, as we in ourselves have nothing that would help anyone connect with Jesus. It's wonderful that the truth is we can depend on the Holy Spirit as we continue in Christ, in both our everyday life as well as our ministry assignment. As we walk with Him, as we pray, as we read His Word, and as we engage in community, we can be confident that we will have the guidance, support and empowerment of the Spirit. He can guide our thinking and shape our actions, both in daily life and in our ministry tasks. And we must have confidence in the power of the Spirit to enable us to undertake our part in His Kingdom mission:

> *Now there are varieties of gifts, but the same Spirit; and there are varieties of service, but the same Lord; and there are varieties of activities, but it is the same God who empowers them all in everyone. To each is given the manifestation of the Spirit for the common good. (1 Corinthians 12:4-7)*

As we abide in Him, the Holy Spirit shines through us, showing forth His love, character and power. It is through Him that we can do whatever He asks of us, not relying on our own ability but on His great power! In Him we can live His way, in Him we can do His works. Trust the Lord! Learn to depend and rely upon His strength – and watch what He does through you!

Ask yourself these questions:

Do I really trust that God is with me? Do I truly rely upon the Holy Spirit for everything? How do I adjust my day to do it more?

Pray this prayer:

Father God, thank you for the leading and empowering of your Holy Spirit. Holy Spirit, make Your presence known to me as I walk through my day. Guide me in my thoughts and actions, and use me to do the greater works of Jesus. I trust You. I rely upon You. I depend on You. I pray this in the name of the Father, and of the Son, and of the Holy Spirit. Amen.

Spiritual Disciplines #12

by Mike Chong Perkinson

"I will depend on the empowering presence of the Holy Spirit in my life and ministry."

"Practice makes perfect" is the popular cultural adage. However, it's not true. Practice doesn't make perfect, but practice does make better. Whether you are practicing something that is life giving or not, you will become better at doing whatever you practice daily.

With that in mind, let's consider a daily practice of dependence where we surrender to the empowering presence of the Holy Spirit. In order to do that we need to rearrange our prepositions. That's right, prepositions. After all, theology is possibly more prepositional than propositional (not to negate propositions but to highlight the relationship). More simply, God's love is *FOR* us as He works *IN* us so that He might manifest *THROUGH* us *FOR* others.

At first glance this is right and true. However, one major preposition is missing which tends to alter the first preposition, "for", with a different object. Too many of us start our day seeking to live *FOR* God as His servant. This isn't wrong, but it tends to move us away from living in His empowering presence relationally as a son or daughter. How you ask?

God did not create humanity to be his hired, saved servants on His massive ranch. The Trinity created *FROM* relationship *FOR* relationship. God doesn't need us to do His bidding or His work as the very stones would cry out in praise if humanity didn't. He created us to be *WITH* Him as sons and daughters before ever being servants and stewards. And so, to live in His empowering presence begins with a daily practice of being in relationship with God as His child.

To do this, *practice gratitude daily* and begin with affirmations of gratefulness each day about His love *FOR* you, accept His presence that is now *WITH* you so that you can be *WITH* Him both now and forever. Thank Him for loving you, forgiving you, and accepting you in Christ and then with gratitude accept His delight over you and choose to join Him in living out your God-given destiny.

Ask yourself these questions:

How can I begin my day WITH God instead of FOR God? What truths about being His beloved child do I need to declare over myself daily? What lie(s) keeps me from living WITH God?

Pray this prayer:

Lord, I begin my day grateful for Your forever love, grace and forgiveness. I rejoice and humbly accept my place as Your child, fully redeemed and empowered to live as You have created me to live. And so, I give all I am to You so that I can be all You want me to be. May Your Kingdom delight and purpose find its full expression in me today wherever I go, in whatever I say and in whatever I do. Amen.

Spiritual Disciplines #13

by Tim McGinnin Jr.

"I will depend on the empowering presence of the Holy Spirit in my life and ministry."

> *As a deer pants for flowing streams, so pants my soul for you, O God. My soul thirsts for God, for the living God. (Psalm 42:1-2a)*

Have you ever worked too long outside in the heat of summer without having a drink? The feeling of a long draw of cold water after doing yardwork or any other physical activity is incredibly satisfying! The moments before I get to that refreshing sip, is usually when I realize just how much I need it. The longer I go without, the more desperate my body feels the need for the hydration. The writer of this psalm captures the desperate need that we all have for the Lord's presence in our lives. Even as our physical bodies crave the sustenance of hydration, so our souls crave the presence of God. The need is acute and constant and there isn't anything that will satisfy apart from the very presence of the living God through the Holy Spirit.

The need for the empowering presence of the Holy Spirit is always there. We are *always in a state of need for the Lord to be present and working in our lives.* The good news is that through Christ, we have the Holy Spirit living in us, so we have unfettered access to the One who is the source of all fulfillment and life for our souls. How good God is to provide for us Himself in this way! The thing is, while our access to the living God is unlimited, it must still be tapped into. We must be intentional about our choices around engaging with the Lord and fully depending on Him for every aspect of our entire lives. In the Beatitudes, Jesus says "Blessed are the poor in spirit, for theirs is the kingdom of heaven" (Matthew 5:3). It is in our understanding and embrace of our desperate need for the Lord, our utter dependence on Him, that we will we make the choice to depend on Him fully in our lives. Even as our bodies remind us when we are hungry or thirsty, *our souls remind us of our need for the Lord* working in and through us. Even as we must make the choice to eat and drink to nourish ourselves physically, we must *make the choice* to depend on the Lord through the empowering presence of the Holy Spirit. Otherwise, we will find ourselves spiritually starving and malnourished.

Ask yourself these questions:

What does it look like for me to recognize my spiritual need for the Lord? How can I remind myself of my need for Him continually so that I live my life in a posture of dependence on Him?

Pray this prayer:

Lord, I need You. I need You for every aspect of my life. I am utterly desperate for Your presence working in and through me. Without You, I can accomplish nothing that is good. Help me to always know and embrace my dependence and need of You. Nourish my soul, Lord and may the life that You give me through Your Spirit flow out in blessing to others and Kingdom advancement all around me. I pray this in the name of the Father, and of the Son, and of the Holy Spirit. Amen.

Spiritual Disciplines #14

by Selina McGinnin

"I will depend on the empowering presence of the Holy Spirit in my life and ministry."

But the Counselor, the Holy Spirit, whom the Father will send in my name, will teach you all things and will remind you of everything I have said to you. (John 14:26)

Take a moment and think about something you use every day. Your arms, your mouth, your legs, etc. Now picture yourself completing a specific task that needs one of those items? Now ask yourself another question. How often do you forget something? Why you walked into a room, the specific address somewhere, what you did yesterday, or that person's name that you just met? Those moments are all too familiar, aren't they?

My point is this, we are a dependent and forgetful people! We need certain tools and people to accomplish tasks (I know how to do taxes but I do not know how to repair the brakes on my car.) Often, we also need reminders. We use calendars, post-it notes, technology, and other means to keep us on track with where we are supposed to be and when.

If this is the case, how foolish and arrogant would we be to think we knew so much and could remember all things that we wouldn't need the gift of the Holy Spirit's presence to lead us in life? Going through life without the continual guidance and empowerment that comes only through the Holy Spirit would be like trying to drive your car with no visibility and no idea where you are.

The Holy Spirit inspires us, guides us, teaches us, tells us when to speak up and when to be quiet, when to go and when to stay. He reminds us who we are, *Whose* we are, and what we are called for and to. In a world telling us who we are and aren't we so easily forget we are sons and daughters of the King. Dependent living on the Holy Spirit means we are continually reminded of the Truth. We gain confidence, stability, and understanding. Imagine walking out life that way? For many of us, it would be a huge difference to the life we walk now.

In every moment we must be aware of the His Presence. Listening, asking, dependent, and responding. There isn't a situation you will ever find yourself in that He is not there with you. The more frequent you talk with Him the more you learn His voice and His ways. Through Him we gain insight and wisdom. We are dependent and forgetful. He is trustworthy and faithful.

Ask yourself these questions:

In what areas of my life do I depend on myself or others more than I trust the Holy Spirit?
How can I start depending on Him in these areas of my life?

Pray this prayer:

Lord, I recognize my need for You. I admit that I am dependent on You, God, to change my heart to trust in you before anything or anyone else. Holy Spirit, fill me and guide me. Teach me to hear Your voice. Amen.

Spiritual Disciplines #15

by Marjorie Clark

"I will depend on the empowering presence of the Holy Spirit in my life and ministry."

But you will receive power when the Holy Spirit has come upon you, and you will be my witnesses... And they were all filled with the Holy Spirit and began to speak in other tongues as the Spirit gave them utterance. (Acts 1:8a; 2:4) But the fruit of the Spirit is love, joy, peace, patience, kindness, goodness, faithfulness, gentleness, self-control; against such things there is no law. And those who belong to Christ Jesus have crucified the flesh with its passions and desires. If we live by the Spirit, let us also keep in step with the Spirit. (Galatians 5:22-25)

For the first 20 years of my life as a child of God, I knew nothing of the Holy Spirit's power in my life. I was saved in a church that taught that the Spirit only pointed to Christ (so we shouldn't focus on the Spirit) and that the manifestations of the Spirit ended with the completion of the canon of Scripture. If I had resident within me power to live the Christian life, I didn't know how to plug into it. I loved God, loved the Word of God and tried with all my strength to obey Him. Ultimately, I failed. Two children and one divorce later I walked away from God because, I thought, I had failed Him and He had failed me. The answer had been in front of me the whole time, but I read it (The Word) through the eyes of my incomplete theology. Then, after 5 years of desert wandering, I encountered the Father's love, was filled with the Holy Spirit, and the Word came alive!

The Holy Spirit is the Helper and the Counselor and the One who is our Teacher – He is also the one I usually *hear* as I go through my day and He directs my steps, my thoughts, my prayers, my words, my understanding ... He is the one who *convicts me* when

I sin (in thought, word, or action – sometimes all three) and reveals the root behind my sin. He *reminds me* that I'm forgiven and loved. He exposes lies that I've believed, and highlights God's truth about who I am, why God created me, and what His purposes are in my life. When I'm praying for someone, He *directs my prayer* to what the Lord is doing in that person's life. He is the source of my faith, wisdom, and compassion. He *directs my steps*. He is my strength. Everything I need to live and serve comes through Him from the Father and the Son. In the years since I was filled with the Spirit, I have grown more and more dependent on Him for every part of my life and ministry. I understand now, more than ever, why Jesus was insistent that His disciples "wait for the Promise of the Father." (Acts 1:4)

Ask yourself these questions:

How is what I believe about the Holy Spirit evident in my life? What is the Spirit saying to me right now that I need to pay attention to?

Pray this prayer:

Father, thank you for sending the Promised Holy Spirit. You keep Your promises! You have provided everything I need to live according to Your Word, and to be Your witness in this world. I know I don't always rely on You, on Your Holy Spirit living in me. Holy Spirit, You are my teacher. Teach me to listen to You and to walk in Your fullness in my life and as I serve others. I ask this believing in You, in the name of the Father, the Son, and the Holy Spirit. Amen.

Spiritual Disciplines #16

by Dr. Tom Johnston

"I am devoted to The Fellowship—living a shared life together in Christ as family and community."

And they devoted themselves to the apostles' teaching and the fellowship, to the breaking of bread and the prayers. (Acts 2:42)

There is a big difference between commitment and devotion. Commitment is a promise to do something in the future, whereas devotion is loyalty and deep affection for a person. Commitment comes from the head; devotion comes from the heart. Commitment is based on a particular situation or agenda; devotion is driven solely by love. Before His crucifixion, the disciples of Jesus were committed to Him based on their agenda – Him restoring national Israel to its former glory. When that didn't happen, they all bailed on Him, even denying Him. But once Christ had risen and the Holy Spirit had transformed their hearts, they became truly devoted, with a passionate loyalty to Christ (the Person), His Church (His people) and His mission (His purpose). Their commitment died with their agenda, but now their devotion would never die. In fact, all but John would lose their lives because of their devotion.

What we see in the Book of Acts is that these Spirit-filled followers of Christ were devoted to one another, loving, caring for and serving one another. They devoted themselves to the fellowship, the people, not just the action of being together. Although, such togetherness was a reflection of their devotion. They met together to worship, to learn, to care for one another's practical needs, and to share resources. Basically, out of their devotion *they did life together*. Life and mission were integrated, the miraculous happened and they did it all as they walked together in daily life. And because of their devotion to one another *the church grew*:

> *And day by day, attending the temple together and breaking bread in their homes, they received their food with glad and generous hearts, praising God and having favor with all the people. And the Lord added to their number day by day those who were being saved. (Acts 2:46-47)*

When we live life together in Christ as a spiritual family and community, we can see the fruit of spiritual growth and multiplication that would never occur through our own commitment. *Devotion is the key*, as we live together devoted to Christ, His Church and His mission. Move beyond commitment, leave your agenda behind, give your heart to the fellowship – be devoted!

Ask yourself these questions:

Am I really devoted to the people in my church? Am I really living in community with them?

Pray this prayer:

Father God, thank You for the people in my life who are Your Church. Holy Spirit, increase my loving devotion to them, loving them with the heart of Jesus. Help me make room in my life to live in community with them. I pray this in the name of the Father, and of the Son, and of the Holy Spirit. Amen.

Spiritual Disciplines #17

by Mike Chong Perkinson

"I am devoted to the fellowship, living a shared life together in Christ as family and community."

We were created from relationship for relationship. The Triune God, who exists in fullness as the Father, the Son and the Spirit - a beautiful relationship of mutuality that is love - exemplifies for us what it means to live in harmony, unity and community. We were created in His image as an "us" that is male and female, a community of people who live in covenant love. Scripture says God is love (FYI, not love is God). We were not created to be independent nor co-dependent; both are results and realities of a fallen and sin-filled world. Were created to be dependent upon God first and foremost for it is "in Him we live and move and have our being." (Acts 17:28) We are penultimate beings and God is the Ultimate Being of the universe where our life force comes from and in and through whom our lives are sustained. It is only in and through Christ that we find ourselves restored to the fullness of His original design.

Humanity struggles with wanting to be known while simultaneously fearing it. We hunger for human connection, love and community but often undermine it because of our woundedness that is housed in fear, shame and anxiety. As a result, we live *in*dependent lives, telling ourselves that we don't need anyone or *co*-dependent lives, determined and defined by others as our shame and fear tell us that we are nobodies unless somebody affirms us. Both postures are hellish and damaging to our souls and keep us from the beauty of healing and restorative community.

There is no healing without community for it requires the presence of another. There is no healing breakthrough without confession and that to another (James 5:16). We are only as free as our ability to confess and own our sin and struggle, no more and no less. You can't change what you won't own or don't know. May you find a community of saints, a godly individual(s) who will lead you into His fullness and call out the Jesus within you (Gal. 4:19).

Ask yourself these questions:

How can I relate more to God as my Father? What fears keep me from engaging more with others? What lies in my past are shaping my present? How can I release those lies and live to the truth of who God says I am?

Pray this prayer:

Lord, I begin my day grateful for Your healing and restorative grace that always meets me right where I am. I pray that Your healing freedom jettisons that child You've created me to be to rise up in faith and live in the fullness of Your delight and purpose. I choose today to surrender my fears, shame and anxiety to You to be replaced and displaced by the healing and freeing grace of Christ. I renounce the lies spoken over me and humbly and joyfully accept the truths You have spoken over in and through Christ. And so, I give all I am to You so that I can be all You want me to be. May Your Kingdom delight and purpose find its full expression in me today wherever I go, in whatever I say and in whatever I do. Amen.

Spiritual Disciplines #18

by Tim McGinnin Jr.

"I am devoted to The Fellowship—living a shared life together in Christ as family and community."

> *While he was still speaking to the people, behold, his mother and his brothers stood outside, asking to speak to him. But he replied to the man who told him, "Who is my mother, and who are my brothers?" And stretching out his hand toward his disciples, he said, "Here are my mother and my brothers! For whoever does the will of my Father in heaven is my brother and sister and mother." (Matthew 12:46-50)*

Jesus' words would have been staggering to everyone around him in this moment and may have been offensive to his mother and brothers who were seeking him out amidst the crowd. He was certainly using this moment to make a critical point about priorities in the Kingdom of God. For the Jews of His time, honoring your family, especially your parents, was incredibly important. Many even regarded the commandment to honor your father and mother as the most important of the Ten Commandments that had to do with relating to others. Jesus was not negating the importance of biological family here but rather He was deconstructing and reconstructing a worldview. He even re-emphasized his value and honor of his mother in John 19:25-27 when, at His crucifixion and close to death, He charged John to care for Mary when He said: "Woman, behold, your son!" Then he said to the disciple, "Behold, your mother!" Jesus taught us that the highest priority in all of life is the Kingdom of God and thus anyone who pursues the Lord's will is to be counted as family.

Many followers of Jesus have biological family members who do not know the Lord. They may even be the only one in their family who is a disciple of Jesus. This can be a challenging situation that creates tension and division amongst households and extended families. Jesus foresaw this and told His disciples that this will be the case (Luke 12:52-53). Yet every disciple of Christ can be sure that regardless of where they stand with the families they grew up with, they have a family in Christ with fellow believers.

The family of the Kingdom of God living life together with the common values and pursuits of loving God, loving others, and making disciples is what advances the Kingdom of God (see Acts 2:42-47). Jesus told us that it is the love that we have for each other as His disciples that will communicate to the world that we belong to Him (John 13:35). This is a significant aspect of our witness as well as our own personal growth as His disciples. When we lean into the family of God that He has given us in community, we better emulate Him and better accomplish His mission.

Ask yourself these questions:

How do I demonstrate being devoted to the Fellowship? How do I share my life with others in community? In what ways is the Lord calling me to invest in the family of the Kingdom through my church community?

Pray this prayer:

Lord, thank You for the Kingdom family that You have given me! Help me to fully embrace living a shared life with others as family and community. Help me to lean into relationships that will advance the Kingdom of God because of my participation. Lord, show me where I need to grow in devotion to The Fellowship and help me to respond with obedient action. I pray this in the name of the Father, and of the Son, and of the Holy Spirit. Amen.

Spiritual Disciplines #19

by Selina McGinnin

"I am devoted to The Fellowship – living a shared life together in Christ as family and community."

In "Star Wars: Rise of Skywalker" there is a scene where Poe Dameron and his fleet from the New Republic (the good guys) are face to face with the First Order (the big bad guys of the movie) and it looks like it's over. The bad guys have a bigger ship, more ships, more fire power and they have the good guys surrounded and are taking out the good guys' ships one by one. Poe, looking defeated, apologizes to his fleet and says there are just too many of them. Then you hear through the radio another voice "But there are more of us." BOOM. Hundreds of ships filled with friends and allies of the good guys, devoted to the mission and its people, come blasting in from hyper speed. Pop, pop, pop. Suddenly it's the bad guys who are outnumbered and surrounded. Hope restored. Encouragement poured out. Back up arrived and the New Republic won the battle. Oh man, this scene made the hair on my arms stand up and admittedly I was a little teary-eyed.

I've been there. Where it felt like the big bad was bigger than me, more powerful than me, and certainly way more equipped than me. The good news, I had back up. The good news is YOU have back up! We are surrounded by encouragers, people who remind us of Hope and Truth. They help provide for our needs, lend a listening ear, provide a safe place to stay, and fight beside us. This is the Church. The Church living out the love and commands of Jesus displays the fullness of God. God created community for us to be surrounded by people who could stand beside us and walk with us through all of life's trials. He knew we could not do it on our own. It was all part of His plan. We need Him; Father, Son and Holy Spirit and we need His Church. We need those around us who are on the same mission, fighting for the same King, pursuing freedom together. Ecclesiastes 4:9-12 tells us the strength we have when we are together with one another and God:

> *Two are better than one, because they have a good reward for their toil. For if they fall, one will lift up his fellow. But woe to him who is alone when he falls and has not another to lift him up! Again, if two lie together, they keep warm, but how can one keep warm alone? And though a man might prevail against one who is alone, two will withstand him—a threefold cord is not quickly broken.*

It is so important that we find the people of God who embody who God called them to be. It is even more important that we live out who God called us to be so we can be devoted to one another and lift one another up. I know some of us have experienced hurt by the church and I don't dismiss that. Scripture still calls us to one another and to love and care for one another, to be in fellowship. If one of us does not live out love it is not for us to bring to justice or abandon the Church altogether. It is cause for us to forgive, reconcile and, if able, allow God to be judge and reconciler, and for us to pursue the Fellowship of the Church no matter what. We are called to it so we must never run from it.

The Community of the Church is our back up, those engaged in battle for us and with us, those who lift us up. We need one another. It changes the fight and the journey completely when we are engaged in fellowship with a community of believers. Like the scene in Star Wars, when we find ourselves up against something that seems too big to take on, we soon realize we have the back up of God through His people surrounding us in battle and we cannot lose.

Ask yourself these questions:

Am I devoted to the Fellowship of the Church? Am I present? Do I encourage and lift up my brothers and sisters?

Have I been hurt by the Church? If so, is it keeping me from en-

gaging and have I fully forgiven?

Pray this prayer:

Father, thank you for being my back up and creating a Community where I am never alone and can receive support. Lord help me to be fully devoted to the Fellowship of the Church, providing support, encouragement and presence. Finally, Lord, please forgive me where I have neglected being present for Your people. Grow me in Your love for Your people. Amen.

Spiritual Disciplines #20

by John Kimball

"I am devoted to The Fellowship – living a shared life together in Christ as family and community."

That which we have seen and heard we proclaim also to you, so that you too may have fellowship with us; and indeed our fellowship is with the Father and with his Son Jesus Christ. And we are writing these things so that our joy may be complete. (1 John 1:3-4)

Devotion to the Fellowship of Believers is an essential of the Christian life. Devotion is relational, not just intellectual. We are to live life and do ministry together – in relationship as a body, a family. As the Apostle John writes his first letter to the Church, he strives to express his wonder at having met, surrendered to, and ministered with the Author of Life Himself. This one thing alone sets Christ's followers apart from the rest of humanity and unto our special community – having met and surrendered to Jesus.

If we are truly devoted to Jesus, this will necessarily lead to devotion to each other. It's hard to understand how a local congregation can function as a gathering of *separate* people, each with their own agenda. It is evidence that real devotion to Jesus must be lacking. For when we love our Triune God with every fiber of our being, we will indeed love each other rightly.

And so, we proclaim this fact to each other – just as John does in his letter. We remind each other of this critical discipline and hold each other lovingly accountable when something isn't working. We practice gospel reconciliation when relationships are broken and strive to live in peace with each other, on the same mission together. And in doing so we actually grow into the very unity of fellowship we seek. It makes our joy complete.

Ask yourself these questions:

Am I an "independent" in the midst of my church family – a "Lone Ranger"? Do I have stressed or broken relationships with other believers that need my immediate attention? Am I experiencing the exquisite joy of real fellowship – remaining on mission together with my church family?

Pray this prayer:

Jesus, I desire to live in real fellowship with my brothers and sisters in the Faith. I know my own propensity toward independence, and even the ways I sometimes stress and wound my relationships with others. Help me by your Spirit to overcome these things by authentic devotion toward other believers. Help me to practice regular reconciliation and to participate in fruitful partnership for Your glory. Amen.

Spiritual Disciplines #21

by Dr. Tom Johnston

"I am devoted to The Breaking of Bread—the celebration of the Lord's Supper and the practice of hospitality."

And they devoted themselves to the apostles' teaching and the fellowship, to the breaking of bread and the prayers. (Acts 2:42)

When Jesus instituted what we call the Lord's Supper, or Communion, He did it around the dinner table at the Passover Supper. It was a very intimate, relational setting normally reserved for family and close friends. It was a time of inclusion, an invitation to share a deeply spiritual moment together. Even as He was the ultimate Passover Lamb (ref. 1 Corinthians 5:7), the complete and final sacrifice (ref. Hebrews 7:27), His time with His disciples at the table was meant as a means of embrace.

Likewise, when we celebrate the Lord's Supper together, we are not just remembering what Christ has done for us on the Cross, but we also join Him in including one another in our lives. As the Trinity made room for us with them through Christ, in Communion we remember to make room for others with us. As we embrace the sacrifice of Christ, we embrace our brothers and sisters who have also been redeemed through His body and blood. We are one body with Him as we partake of His body, and we drink of the same cup of the Covenant with Him, and also with one another. As we devote ourselves to Christ through His Supper, we devote ourselves to life together with those with whom we share His body and His blood.

In the same way, when we open our homes, we invite those with whom we share covenant in entering into a shared life in Christ – moving beyond the moment of ritual into the fullness of everyday life. True community is lived out as our covenant with

Christ and His people when it takes on real form in real life. We are devoted when we open our hearts, our homes and our lives to others in His body, demonstrating acceptance, inclusion, and embrace – the very same things we have already received from Him. Be devoted to His table, and open yours to others as a living demonstration of His loving devotion to us!

Ask yourself these questions:

Do I see the Lord's table as an act of devotion to Christ and His Church? DO I invite people into my life, my home, my table?

Pray this prayer:

Father God, thank You for the gift of acceptance and inclusion You have given me through the body and blood of Jesus Christ. Holy Spirit, free me to embrace and include the people of my church family, making room for them in my life. I pray this in the name of the Father, and of the Son, and of the Holy Spirit. Amen.

Spiritual Disciplines #22

by Mike Chong Perkinson

"I am devoted to The Breaking of Bread – the celebration of the Lord's Supper and the practice of hospitality."

Sacraments are beautiful as they are "holy signs and seals of the covenant of grace" by which we encounter the amazing and life-giving grace of God. The sacrament of the Lord's Supper, the meal shared by the early church in commemoration of the risen Lord, beautifully captures the healing that comes by way of the Cross. It is a celebration of the restored ones at a common table that is founded upon Passover.

First Passover in Egypt. The final event that released the Jews from Egypt was the sacrifice of an unblemished lamb whose bones could not be broken either in preparation or even after death which would render the sacrifice invalid. The blood of the lamb was placed on the doorposts of the houses and those within the house were protected from death. It took an act of faith to do that. Those who did, including Egyptians, were saved from death.

Passover continues to be celebrated in Jewish communities. Over the years, this came to include four different cups of wine.

1. The Cup of Sanctification – based on God's statement, "I will bring you out from under the burdens of the Egyptians"
2. The Cup of Judgment or Deliverance – based on God's statement, "I will deliver you from slavery to them"
3. The Cup of Redemption – based on God's statement, "I will redeem you with an outstretched arm"
4. The Cup of Praise or Restoration – based on God's statement, "I will take you to be my people, and I will be your God"

The third cup of wine represents the redeeming blood of the lamb. In Jewish thought wine represents blood and joy. In the days of judgment on Egypt, Moses turned the water into blood. This was a foreshadowing of the coming Messiah, who would be like Moses, and would do something similar. The rabbis, the sages of old, said that when Messiah comes, He would be able to take water and turn it into wine because it would no longer be a time of judgment but of joy. This is highly significant when you recall Yeshua's first miracle at the wedding in Cana – turning the water into wine.

At the last Passover Jesus celebrated with His disciples, He took the cup after supper, which would have been the 3rd cup in the ceremony – the one that represents the lamb's blood -- and Jesus identified His work. Jesus said, "this cup represents my blood." This would have been quite shocking.

There is another ceremony that is more than 2000 years old and is still practiced in some communities today. When a young man is interested in a young lady, an arrangement is made by the fathers including a ceremony that cements their relationship into a legally binding marriage. The young man brings a cup of wine to the bride-to-be and says to her, "The wine in this goblet is representative of my life's blood, if you drink this wine, you'll be mine. You'll be married to me." If she takes the cup and drinks it, they are officially married in betrothal to each other.

What we have in the Lord's Supper is an overlaying of two ceremonies: at the last Passover Messiah was indeed fulfilling the Passover tradition as well as making a marriage proposal to His disciples. A bride who became married in this fashion did not immediately move into the house with her husband - this simply began the betrothal period which could last a year or two.

The bridegroom would return to the home of his father and begin to build a place suitable for his bride, guided by his father who knew what the bride would want. When the home was done, the bridegroom would go and get his bride. This was often done at night in a torch lit procession. The bride would have approximated the time of his coming, gifts having been sent to her from the bridegroom as well as correspondence, and she, having prepared herself in readiness for his arrival, would joyously meet him.

They would not drink of the fruit of the vine until they could do it together. The secondary purpose of wine is joy and so, their joy would never be complete until they could do it together. Which is why Jesus said "I will not drink of the fruit of the vine again until I can drink it with you in My Father's kingdom."

The penalty in the Torah for adultery is death which sheds light on why the apostle Paul said, "some of you are eating and drinking unworthily causing some to be sick and even die." We are betrothed in marriage to the Lord and so we don't flirt with the lifestyle and the ways of the world.

Ask yourself these questions:

1. ***Am I living as one betrothed to the Lord?***
2. ***Are there ways in which I am "eating and drinking" of the Lord's Supper in an unworthy manner?***
3. ***How have I lived mutually with others, inviting them to the table of fellowship in my home and daily life?***
4. ***In what ways am I looking forward to (preparing myself in readiness) the Groom's return for the ultimate celebration and feast at the Marriage Supper of the Lamb?***

Pray this prayer:

Lord, I am humbled that you chose me as I did not choose You. Thank You for seeking me out and loving me even when I have been faithless and unfaithful. Help me today to live in the fullness of covenant love as I choose to follow You today and love You with my whole life, and love others as You have loved me. I choose to invite people to the table of fellowship where we sit in mutuality

breaking bread and honoring the Christ who has restored our lives, and offering healing hospitality to all I come in contact with today. Amen.

Spiritual Disciplines #23

by Dr. Tom Johnston

"I am devoted to The Breaking of Bread—the celebration of the Lord's Supper and the practice of hospitality."

In those days a decree went out from Caesar Augustus that all the world should be registered. This was the first registration when Quirinius was governor of Syria. And all went to be registered, each to his own town. And Joseph also went up from Galilee, from the town of Nazareth, to Judea, to the city of David, which is called Bethlehem, because he was of the house and lineage of David, to be registered with Mary, his betrothed, who was with child. And while they were there, the time came for her to give birth. And she gave birth to her firstborn son and wrapped him in swaddling cloths and laid him in a manger, because there was no place for them in the inn. (Luke 2:1-7)

It might surprise you to know that the issue of hospitality is a main theme in the Gospel of Luke. It starts right at the beginning of the story with the birth of Jesus. The manner of the birth of the King is symbolic of the ongoing rejection: the One who should have been welcomed with open arms and great fanfare had to sleep with the animals. Such a reception of the King of kings was quite inhospitable! It wasn't until the shepherds showed up some time later that anyone was present to receive Him in proper fashion. And they all marveled at the setting in which they find the Messiah! All of this is indicative of the human rejection of God – and how, in response, He sought us out through the incarnation of Christ.

When we practice hospitality, welcoming people into our homes, into our lives, then we exemplify the Father's love which He has shown us in Christ:

Therefore welcome one another as Christ has welcomed you, for the glory of God. (Romans 15:7)

Too often we either isolate and exclude people, or we have a far too casual approach to our hosting of others. We should open our homes to one another, practicing hospitality as the Scripture instructs us to do (ref. Acts 28:7, Romans 12:13, 1 Timothy 3:2, 1 Timothy 5:10, Titus 1:8, Hebrews 13:2, 1 Peter 4:9). It is in this action that we model and express the inclusion, acceptance and embrace which the Lord has extended to us. We need to make room for Jesus in His people in our homes and in our lives!

Ask yourself these questions:

How well am I practicing hospitality? What could I do differently to show God's acceptance through being hospitable to others?

Pray this prayer:

Father God, thank You that You have welcomed me in Christ. Holy Spirit, show me how You would have me practice hospitality so that others might experience Your acceptance through me. I pray this in the name of the Father, and of the Son, and of the Holy Spirit. Amen.

Spiritual Disciplines #24

by Tim McGinnin Jr.

"I am devoted to The Breaking of Bread—the celebration of the Lord's Supper and the practice of hospitality."

In Luke 24, the very first Resurrection Sunday, we read about the account of two disciples having an encounter with Jesus while they were making the seven mile walk from Jerusalem to Emmaus. They didn't recognize Him at first. They made their journey in despair about Jesus' death and they explained to the stranger who joined them on the way what kind of tragedy they were dealing with. Jesus responds to them by revealing truth from Scripture about Himself and they still do not recognize Him. The journey culminates at their destination with the two disciples inviting Jesus in for the night as their cultural norms for hospitality would have required them to do. They all settled in and sat down for the evening meal:

> *When he [Jesus] was at table with them, he took the bread and blessed and broke it and gave it to them. And their eyes were opened, and they recognized him. And he vanished from their sight. They said to each other, "Did not our hearts burn within us while he talked to us on the road, while he opened to us the Scriptures?" (Luke 24:30-32)*

It's amazing that Jesus reveals Himself to these two disciples in the breaking of the bread at the table together. Jesus had broken bread like this before during the miraculous feedings of the 4,000 and 5,000 (Matthew 13:14-21, 15:32-38), as well as during the Last Supper (Matthew 26:26-29). In fact, during His last meal with His disciples, He indicated that they should take the broken bread and the cup in remembrance of Him, initiating the practice of Communion that we still partake in today. In this instance, for these two disciples, Jesus wasn't just remembered in the breaking of the bread but was actually revealed and recognized by His two followers. This encounter with the Risen Lord rejuvenated them immediately to the point where they left their home right away and went back to Jerusalem to tell the remaining eleven apostles and those who were with them about Jesus' resurrection and their encounter with Him (Luke 24:33-35).

When we come to the Lord's Table in Communion, it is certainly a time of remembrance and reflection as Jesus indicated it should be. This remembrance though should not just be for the past: regarding Jesus earthly ministry, death for our sins, and defeat of death in His resurrection; but it should also be an active celebration and encounter with the living God who continues to live in and through us through the power and presence of the Holy Spirit. I invite you to partake in Communion today with this perspective and may He be revealed to you afresh in the breaking of bread and the drinking of the cup.

Ask yourself these questions:

How have I experienced the Lord's presence through partaking in Communion? How has the practice of Communion helped me to refocus and/or re-center on Jesus amidst the various circumstances of life?

Pray this prayer:

Lord, reveal Yourself to me in the breaking of bread. Help me to not simply passively remember You in the practice of Communion, but may I actively encounter You through this discipline and practice. Lord use this discipline and celebration to help me continually refocus my life on You. Amen

Spiritual Disciplines #25

by Selina McGinnin

"I am devoted to The Breaking of Bread – the celebration of the Lord's Supper and the practice of hospitality."

During supper, when the devil had already put it into the heart of Judas Iscariot, Simon's son, to betray him, Jesus, knowing that the Father had given all things into his hands, and that he had come from God and was going back to God, rose from supper. He laid aside his outer garments, and taking a towel, tied it around his waist. Then he poured water into a basin and began to wash the disciples' feet and to wipe them with the towel that was wrapped around him. (John 13:2-5)

There is a costly step in opening ourselves up to others. When we open ourselves up to someone, we give them a chance to hurt us, we allow ourselves to be vulnerable. In John's gospel we read that Jesus, who had opened Himself in relationship with His disciples, including Judas, was sitting at the Passover meal and was preparing to wash their feet. Jesus already had full knowledge of the turmoil that He was about to enter into as He journeyed to the cross. He also knew who was going to betray Him and turn Him in. It would be Judas, one of His disciples who He invited into relationship and whose feet He washed. Yet, even with this knowledge (and since He is Jesus, He knew this all along) He STILL sets out to wash the disciples' feet, even Judas. Furthermore, Judas was invited to a seat at the table with Jesus. This is the true practice of hospitality. It is the ministry of embracing the other by allowing those whom are not like us and may have even betrayed us to be with us. We allow ourselves to be vulnerable for the sake of God being glorified.

If others are to hear the message of the Gospel, we must allow them a seat at our table. They must be served by our hands just as Judas was served by Jesus. They must be cared for gently in the midst of a world filled with contempt and hatred even if, like Judas, they are the ones perpetrating it. Jesus embraces those regardless of the "truth" the world says about them. He cares only that they belong to the Father. There are so many "truths" we believe about people because of what we have heard, what we have been taught, or what sometimes the person puts on as a front. We must break through those perceptions and learn to embrace all people and welcome them in.

The message and remembrance of the Lord's Supper is that salvation is for all because of One. Forgiveness and justification come through Jesus Christ alone. If it comes from Him alone and He allowed Judas a seat at His table than why do we think we can be justified in excluding someone from ours? If we choose to exclude from our table those who are different or adverse, we miss this exact message! We in fact don't truly celebrate, remember or honor the Lord's Supper and His message of embrace and inclusion for all. Our greatest act of celebrating and remembering is to live out towards one another the same love Jesus had for us on the cross.

Ask yourself these questions:

Judas, though a betrayer, had a seat at the table and he had clean feet. Who is your Judas that needs to be invited to your table? Who have you been excluding that God is asking you to begin embracing and what are the first steps you can take towards the act of inclusion? Pray for that person, now!

Pray this prayer:

Jesus, thank you for your example of hospitality and inclusion by showing us how to include the outcasts and those who would persecute us. Father, give us your wisdom to know when to pursue and when to wait in relationships. Open doors for restoration so that

we may practice and share the message of the Last Supper and the Cross. We are grateful to you, Lord, for your love and devotion to all of God's children. Amen.

Spiritual Disciplines #26

Part 1

by Dr. Tom Johnston

"I will practice generosity through tithing as a means of personal discipline, giving offerings as an act of love and providing for the needs of others."

This affirmation of the C.O.D.E. has three elements which comprise a larger view of generosity. I will break it down in three separate devotionals, starting with tithing.

The word tithe simply means *one tenth* of something. It has always been a means of honoring God as the source of our provision. It is established in the Bible when Abraham gives Melchizedek ten percent of the spoils of a battle (ref. Genesis 14:20). Abraham did this because Melchizedek was a priest of God Most High. So, in this action, Abraham was not just honoring Melchizedek, but he was honoring God as the source of his victory and provision. In the New Testament, it says of Jesus "You are a priest forever, after the order of Melchizedek" (Hebrews 7:17). Melchizedek is a type, or a foreshadowing, of Christ in the Old Testament. Abraham was actually honoring Christ through his tithe without even knowing it!

With the Law of Moses, the tithe became a part of the expectation God had for ancient Israel. In fact, if you added up all the giving the Law called for, it came to over 23 percent! Now we are no longer under the Law, but the principle of tithing was established before the Law and was affirmed by Jesus in the New Testament (Luke 11:42). In this passage Jesus corrected the Pharisees for doing the minimum requirement of tithing, but neglecting to love others! Tithing is a basic spiritual discipline and not some kind of advance spiritual practice only a few "super saints" do. I think of it as "the minimum buy-in to the Kingdom of God." It is the least we can do in responding to God's gift of Christ.

Giving one-tenth of our income to the Lord is a means of honoring the Lord, but it is also spiritual practice which helps us discipline ourselves with the use of our finances. In tithing we recognize God as the source of our provision, and remind ourselves that the skills we possess, our education, the jobs we have, all our opportunities to earn income have their source in Him:

> *Beware lest you say in your heart, 'My power and the might of my hand have gotten me this wealth.' You shall remember the LORD your God, for it is he who gives you power to get wealth, that he may confirm his covenant that he swore to your fathers, as it is this day. (Deuteronomy 8:17-18)*

How we use what He provides matters to Him. Money serves as "spiritual training wheels" for being entrusted with the "true riches" of the Kingdom of God:

> *"One who is faithful in a very little is also faithful in much, and one who is dishonest in a very little is also dishonest in much. If then you have not been faithful in the unrighteous wealth, who will entrust to you the true riches? And if you have not been faithful in that which is another's, who will give you that which is your own? No servant can serve two masters, for either he will hate the one and love the other, or he will be devoted to the one and despise the other. You cannot serve God and money." (Luke 16:10-13)*

Do you want the Lord to entrust to you the greater things of the kingdom? Then learn to use your money according to His will. Begin with tithing, and watch how the Lord blesses you with the "true riches" of His Kingdom!

Ask yourself these questions:

Do I use the resources God has given me according to His will and

for His purposes? Am I consistent and faithful to tithe on all the financial resources God has entrusted to me?

Pray this prayer:

Father God, thank You for being my provider. All good things come from You. I acknowledge You as my source of financial and spiritual provision. Thank You for the opportunities I have to earn income. Forgive me for not always using Your resources according to Your will. Holy Spirit, I ask that You would guide me in every financial decision I make. I pray this in the name of the Father, and of the Son, and of the Holy Spirit. Amen.

Spiritual Disciplines #27

Part 2

by Dr. Tom Johnston

"I will practice generosity through tithing as a means of personal discipline, giving offerings as an act of love and providing for the needs of others."

This affirmation of the C.O.D.E. has three elements which comprise a larger view of generosity. This is the second of three devotions on the theme, specifically about offerings.

Offerings are an aspect of generous giving which is over and above the Lord's tithe. It is an action which flows from the Lord's love in our hearts in response to a particular need with which we are presented. Even as tithing is an act of loving discipline, offerings are a way of actively going beyond the minimum. They can be regular and consistent like tithing, or they can be in response to a need you are made aware of. Those needs can be of various kinds: *local and global missions, benevolent needs in the church community and beyond, ministry projects, outreach and evangelistic efforts, and building projects* are all common needs frequently addressed through offerings. The Apostle Paul commended the Philippian church for their partnership with him in the work of the Gospel:

> *And you Philippians yourselves know that in the beginning of the gospel, when I left Macedonia, no church entered into partnership with me in giving and receiving, except you only. (Philippians 4:15)*

The Philippians gave to support Paul's missionary efforts, and received the blessing of participating in advancing the Gospel. My wife and I tithe every time we get paid, and then we also set aside our planned offerings. We give to local and global missionaries as well as other ministry organizations that further the Kingdom of God. When we become aware of other particular ministry or benevolent needs, we prayerfully engage the Lord on how we should respond, and give according to His direction. We are "all in" with Jesus and His Kingdom efforts, and this includes the financial and practical resources which He has entrusted to us. Our approach is regular and consistent, but also spontaneous as we see an opportunity to partner with Him in His work of Kingdom extension. We cannot outgive God!

My encouragement for you is to go beyond the minimum and maximize your generosity through giving offerings. The Kingdom work needs the finances the Lord has entrusted to you – so be generous, as He has been generous with you!

Ask these questions:

What Kingdom work could I invest in beyond my tithe? Am I stuck in the minimum of tithing, or am I truly being generous?

Pray this prayer:

Father God, thank You for being my provider. I ask that You would open my eyes and my heart to the opportunities I have around me to invest in Your Kingdom work through giving an offering. Father, I ask for the opportunity to express my love for You, Your Church and Your mission through my financial resources. Holy Spirit, guide me into maximum generosity. I pray this in the name of the Father, and of the Son, and of the Holy Spirit. Amen.

Spiritual Disciplines #28

Part 3

by Dr. Tom Johnston

"I will practice generosity through tithing as a means of personal discipline, giving offerings as an act of love and providing for the needs of others."

This affirmation of the C.O.D.E. has three elements which comprise a larger view of generosity. This is the third of three devotionals on this topic, specifically about generosity through providing for the needs of others.

It's obvious, but we can't "outgive" God. In His generosity, He gave us His only begotten Son as payment for our sin (ref. John 3:16). He saw our need and made provision for it through the death of Christ on the Cross. Likewise, we are always to be aware of the needs around us. In Philippians 2:4 the Apostle Paul says "Let each of you look not only to his own interests, but also to the interests of others." We can often become so self-absorbed that we don't even see what is happening in the lives of those right around us.

We need to understand God's expectation of our responsibility to be generous towards those who have less practical or financial resources than we do. We are to *love our neighbor as ourselves* in real and tangible forms. Caring for others is a demonstration of God's love through us, and a reminder of His generosity to us in Christ. When you give of your time, talent and treasure to meet the real-world needs of others, you acknowledge the Father as the source of your own provision – and that you trust Him to meet your own needs.

Remember, "*Whoever is generous to the poor lends to the LORD, and he will repay him for his deed.*" (Proverbs 19:17) The Father will take care of you as you follow the Holy Spirit's leading to provide someone's practical needs. Sacrificing your own desire or need for something in order to care for the need of someone else is very Christ-like. You don't always need the next upgrade, or the latest and greatest of something. You might consider regularly setting aside some of your income, over and above the Lord's tithe, to care for the practical needs of other people. Then, when a need does arise, you are ready to respond in love.

Look around. See who might have a need that you can meet. Then, ask the Lord to tell you what to do – and then do it! Be generous, as He has been so generous with us through Christ!

Ask yourself these questions:

Am I aware of the needs of those around me? When I am, do I respond in generosity, or am I stingy?

Pray this prayer:

Father God, thank You for being my provider. I ask You for a generous heart – a heart like Yours. Holy Spirit, please open my eyes to the needs of those around me, and open my heart to respond in loving action to care for them. I pray that You would use me and the resources which You have entrusted to me to meet the practical needs of others. I pray this in the name of the Father, and of the Son, and of the Holy Spirit. Amen.

Spiritual Disciplines #29

by Tim McGinnin Jr.

"I will practice generosity through tithing as a means of personal discipline, giving offerings as an act of love and providing for the needs of others."

And my God will supply every need of yours according to his riches in glory in Christ Jesus. (Philippians 4:19)

I can remember one of the first times my family was on the receiving end of Christ-like generosity. I was a teenager living at home and not yet a Christian. My dad had recently become a Christian and was going to church regularly. We were going through some challenging times financially which nobody really knew about. We were a private family when it came to things like that. Unexpectedly, when we were all at home, a man from my dad's church knocked on the door with a van full of food. He helped to coordinate a ministry that provided groceries to families in need. My dad recognized him, but he didn't really know him. He said "Hey, the Lord put your family on my heart today and I thought maybe you'd like some groceries." My dad quietly and gratefully accepted the offer, not really knowing how he could have known that we could indeed use the food. With help from my siblings and I, he proceeded to empty his van of several boxes and bags of groceries for our family. It stocked our fridge and cupboards abundantly. We were stunned and speechless. I don't think we said a whole lot other than thanking him profusely as he left. It would not be the last time he brought us groceries, as he also did for many other families in the church and community. He was a generous man and his devotion of time and resources to others impacted me significantly even before I ever knew the Lord. Since then, I've received and witnessed the sacrificial and compassionate generosity of followers of Jesus innumerable times.

The practice of generosity played out in our lives comes from the reality that we have a generous God. The longer we walk in relationship with the Lord the more we know Him, and the more we know Him the more we realize how generous and gracious He is. The Lord is faithful to meet the needs of His children and He often does that through other people responding to the generosity of the Lord and 'paying it forward' to others.

Ask yourself these questions:

How have I experienced the generosity of God through other people? How can I demonstrate His sacrificial love and generosity to those around me?

Pray this prayer:

Lord thank You for Your unconditional and perfect love and generosity. Thank You for constantly giving of Yourself to me through the Holy Spirit. Thank you for giving Your Son Jesus on the cross which was the ultimate act of generosity towards those You love. Help me to be generous the way that You are generous. May Your loving generosity flow through me and be poured out to those around me so that You might be glorified and others might come to know You, love You, and walk with You. Amen.

Spiritual Disciplines #30

by Marjorie Clark

"I will practice generosity through tithing as a means of personal discipline, giving offerings as an act of love for the needs of others."

> *Will man rob God? Yet you are robbing me. But you say, 'How have we robbed you?' In your tithes and contributions. You are cursed with a curse, for you are robbing me, the whole nation of you. Bring the full tithe into the storehouse, that there may be food in my house. And thereby put me to the test, says the Lord of hosts, if I will not open the windows of heaven for you and pour down for you a blessing until there is no more need. (Malachi 3:8-10)*

> *And day by day, attending the temple together and breaking bread in their homes, they received their food with glad and generous hearts, (Acts 2:46)*

Initially I struggled to understand the first six words of this affirmation (go ahead, count them), because I didn't connect generosity with tithing. So, I had to go to the Word. As I did, Holy Spirit started connecting the dots for me. Decades ago, as a single mom I struggled with tithing when I started working. Before then it was not my decision to make – it was my husband's. When it became my choice, I took one look at my checkbook and rationalized my way out of God's blessing. Not to mention that I only rarely went to church. But God! The day came when I decided to put Him to the test, no matter what, as I repented of my rebellion and lack of trust and basically handed Him the reins. This began many years of financial struggle and poor stewardship, but persistence in tithing. I longed for the day when I'd be out of debt – because I yearned to be able to give generously. I was tithing, but I wasn't being a faithful steward with the other 90%. "If then you have not been faithful in the unrighteous wealth, who will entrust to you the true riches?" (Luke

16:11)

Those years of personal discipline in tithing (the full 10%) had a hidden benefit – they developed a Spiritual Discipline Muscle (SDM) in me. That SDM then gave me what I needed to create a budget, say "no" to emotional impulse buying, get out (and stay out) of debt, and practice what I call "grateful generosity". In the Acts Scripture above, notice the progression – they were worshipping God together, they received the food shared with them with grateful *and* generous hearts. They weren't just consuming gratefully – no! – they were thinking of others they could share with even as they ate. There have been several times in our home when we made 'too much' food for dinner and the lady of the house said, even as she served it up, "I wonder if the 'Smiths' would like this?" and she'd immediately text them. There's an **immediacy of generosity** flowing from their 'glad hearts'.

Do you understand that generosity honors God? "*Whoever oppresses a poor man insults his Maker, but he who is generous to the needy honors him.*" (Proverbs 14:31) I love that I am able to love others through acts of generosity. And it's a joy to know that God is honored by it.

His master said to him, 'Well done, good and faithful servant. You have been faithful over a little; I will set you over much. Enter into the joy of your master.' (Matthew 25: 21, 21) The relationship between our financial stewardship and our spiritual stewardship is made possible because of the SDM you develop in the discipline of tithing and all that develops from that seemingly 'little' thing. It makes all the difference in the world when coupled with a 'glad and generous heart'. Think about this – the heart is a muscle. A vital muscle. Think "cardio". Really! You can strengthen your heart with the spiritual discipline of tithing.

Ask yourself this question:

What is my next step in strengthening my heart and spirit in the

area of practicing generosity?

Pray this prayer:

Father, You are generous in every way. You give of Your love, Your time ... all of heaven's resources in abundance. You cause the rain to fall on both the just and the unjust. I realize I fall short of imitating You in Your generous heart for people. Far short. I have been ungrateful, not consciously, but in practice I have not received the daily bread You give me with a glad heart. I have not even considered sharing it with others. Thank you for opening my understanding. Show me what to do next, and I will do it ... with a glad and generous heart. I pray this in Your name – Father, Son, and Holy Spirit.

Spiritual Disciplines #31

by Dr. Tom Johnston

"I will lovingly, gently and graciously share with others the story of how God's love and grace has transformed my heart and life."

One thing I do know, that though I was blind, now I see." (John 9:25b)

It might be hard to believe, but the truth is that most people who decide for follow Christ don't do so because of some great sermon or teaching by a pastor. Usually, they come to faith in Christ through someone's personal story about what Jesus has done for them. Now, to be sure, people need good teaching from the Bible to fully know Jesus and follow Him, but it usually starts through someone's story of their own transformation – someone who has a story like you.

In John 9, Jesus healed a man who was born blind. Jesus left before the man received his sight. This fellow didn't know where Jesus was, or who He was, but he considered himself a disciple. When questioned by the religious authorities, the guy didn't really have much information, but what he did have was the transformation that arose from His encounter with Christ: he had been blind, but now he could see.

Like the man who Jesus healed, we don't have all the answers, or even all the information about Jesus. But we do have a story to tell of what Jesus has done for us – and we need to tell it. We have never seen Jesus. We don't know where He is (I know, heaven, but where is that exactly?). We don't have all the doctrinal data points locked down. Yet we call ourselves His disciples and we know that our encounter with Him has transformed us and changed our lives. And we tell our story. How loneliness became belonging, how depression became joy, how addiction became freedom, and how our brokenness became His wholeness. Those are the stories we need to tell, and we need to do it lovingly and gently:

> *...but in your hearts honor Christ the Lord as holy, always being prepared to make a defense to anyone who asks you for a reason for the hope that is in you; yet do it with gentleness and respect, (1 Peter 3:15)*

As you are living unashamedly out loud for Jesus everywhere you go, you can expect people to ask you about, well, *you*. So, tell them your story, your Jesus story of love and transformation. Do it with loving respect and gentleness, answering their questions about you and your experience with Him. Tell them why you have placed your trust and hope in Christ. Share what He has done in you and for you – and then watch what He does through you as you share how His love and grace has transformed your life!

Ask yourself these questions:

Who has been asking me questions about my life? Who needs to hear my Jesus story?

Pray this prayer:

Father God, thank You for my transformation in Christ. Holy Spirit, show me how to share my story with those around me. Lead me to those who need to hear what you have done for me. I pray this in the name of the Father, and of the Son, and of the Holy Spirit. Amen.

Spiritual Disciplines #32

by Mike Chong Perkinson

"I will lovingly, gently and graciously share with others the story of how God's love and grace has transformed my heart and life."

The human heart, naturally and often unconsciously, gives away what is in it. As they say, we reproduce who we are. The seeds for what you will reproduce are in you, both for what is righteous and what is not; what brings life and what does not. When it comes to sharing our faith, the process is simpler than we have allowed it to be. The Apostle Paul helps us here when he tells us that the comfort we have received is the comfort we give (2 Cor 1:4). The key to sharing the love of Christ is not in the simple propositional truths, as important as that might be. Intellectual apologetics is vital and necessary, but these propositions point to the One who is the Truth. The picture and description of your spouse is wonderful and important, but neither are the same as being with them. Is it possible that many saints share a wonderful description of Jesus as they hold up a picture of Him, adoring Him and the truths about Him, but without actually spending time with Him? Hugging a picture and a proposition doesn't bring the same joy as being with the description and the one in the picture. There is then a need for a relational apologetic that shares from its experience with the One in the picture who is the Truth, the Way and the Life. It is in and from this experience where we have been so powerfully loved, gently healed and graciously accepted by our Father in and through Christ that we share from a heart that has been radically comforted by His presence to share with others our story of God's healing and freeing hope. He is with us and that brings a peace and joy like nothing else can.

Sharing our story is vital to our victory as Revelation 12:11 makes clear that we overcome the evil one by the blood of the Lamb, the word of our testimony (our story), and that we do not love our lives over Him. Sharing our story has been frightening for many as they fear they do not know enough theology or Scripture to share the truths about God. What we fail to grasp here is that we have been called to be witnesses of the divine mercies. Witnesses don't tell everything there is to know about a subject, they simply report what they have seen, heard and experienced from their perspective (I Jn 1:1-4). You know, the comfort you have received. You are an expert on your life, a witness to all He has done in your life, continues to do in your life – share it lovingly, gently and graciously to a world that is looking for a real and lived faith that brings a peace this world cannot give. Testify to who you know and how you know Him!

Ask yourself these questions:

1. ***Am I spending time with the propositions and the picture of God more than living in His presence? If so, how do I move into living in His presence daily?***
2. ***What has God saved me from?***
3. ***What am I witness to when it comes to His saving mercies in my life?***
4. ***What is the comfort I have received from God?***

Pray this prayer:

Lord, I am grateful that You have chosen me and saved me. I am moved by the comfort You continue to give me and I want to share the love You have so freely given to me to all I come in contact with today. I am confident in your Spirit that will empower me with the right words to share from my well of comfort for those I encounter today. May I share with loving boldness Your healing mercies today and be a witness to all You have done in my life.

Spiritual Disciplines #33

by Tim McGinnin Jr.

"I will lovingly, gently and graciously share with others the story of how God's love and grace has transformed my heart and life."

> *But in your hearts honor Christ the Lord as holy, always being prepared to make a defense to anyone who asks you for a reason for the hope that is in you; yet do it with gentleness and respect. (1 Peter 3:15)*

Shortly after becoming a Christian as a teenager in high school, I think I misinterpreted this Scripture to mean "always be prepared to be defensive" when it comes to sharing about Jesus. There were times that I pushed my friends away with defensiveness because of my newfound faith. I had to learn that giving a defense for my hope in Christ was very different than being defensive! In an online world full of one-sided opinions and social media arguments, this seems to be more and more common as the times progress and as people become more and more entrenched with the constant and infinite barrage of information and divisive diatribe available for viewing and participation with the swipe of a finger or click of a mouse. Yet, this is not at all what we are called to do. If we read this passage carefully, we see that the apostle Peter is calling us to be prepared to have conversations gently and respectfully with others about why we hope in Christ, specifically when we're asked! This is in stark contrast to much of what we see in comment threads on news sites and various social media platforms.

The approach we take to sharing our personal stories and experiences with God is incredibly important because it influences whether the sharing is heard. More than that, it even influences whether or not we actually share the Gospel through our sharing! Now, we are not responsible for how people respond to our testimonies, but we are responsible for how we treat people in every aspect of our lives. My wife often says, "I don't always remember exactly what people say, but I always remember how they make me feel." I find this to true for most people. Treating others with love, gentleness, and respect is as much part of our story of how God has shaped us, as the words we use to tell the story.

Ask yourself these questions:

Have I ever been defensive in my approach to sharing about the Lord with others? What do I need to work on in how I share my story in terms of being more loving, gentle, and/or respectful in the way I share? Who is the Lord inviting me to be in relationship with right now that may present opportunities to be asked questions about the hope that is in me in Christ?

Pray this prayer:

Lord, help me to always be prepared to give account for the hope that I have in You when I'm asked questions. Empower me by Your Holy Spirit to be like You in those moments of sharing. Help me to emulate the love and graciousness of Christ in a gentle and respectful way. Let not just my words be part of my testimony to others, but the very way I live in You also.

Spiritual Disciplines #34

by Marjorie Clark

"I will lovingly, gently and graciously share with others the story of how God's love and grace has transformed my heart and life."

> *And in that day, declares the Lord, you will call me 'My Husband,' and no longer will you call me 'My Baal.' For I will remove the names of the Baals from her mouth, and they shall be remembered by name no more... I will betroth you to me in righteousness and in justice, in steadfast love and in mercy. I will betroth you to me in faithfulness. And you shall know the Lord. (Hosea 2:16-17, 19-20)*

You may recall the story of the prophet Hosea and Gomer, his bride who had been a prostitute. She could not seem to remain faithful to him, or his God, but continually returned to her "harlotry" and idolatry. I have compassion for Gomer. The culture and religious atmosphere she was raised in gave her no basis for understanding Hosea or Hosea's God. She had a lot to learn about real love – God's love. Though I didn't come from the same background as Gomer, I understand what it's like to be unable to clearly understand the ways of God when looking through the lenses of my upbringing.

Saved at 16, married at 22, two children by 24, divorced at 35. Neither my alcoholic parents, nor my husband's alcoholic and abusive father prepared us for married life and parenting. We tried. We tried hard. I left my husband and children, and my God. I yelled and swore at God so He'd leave me alone. I was afraid He'd make me go back to my verbally and emotionally abusive husband. I quit trying. I shut down emotionally. I let go of restraint, or so I thought. It took two years for the divorce to be finalized. By then my children were living with me, and I had a well-paying job in San Francisco. But life was shaky.

It's funny how you can't really silence God or erase Him from your thoughts. I had worked hard at driving God out of my mind, out of my life. And yet, I recall perfectly the day I was enjoying an ice-cold drink in a café in the city when I heard a clear, quiet voice in the back of my head. "You know it's all true." What? "You know it's all true...about Me...and Jesus." Honestly, I was shocked. I'd have thought the Lord would have given up on me. I was a lost cause. Or, so I thought. He seems to like lost causes. In fact, I'd venture to say He delights in lost causes. It took several years of healing and learning and getting to know this One who loved me so thoroughly and relentlessly, and it continues to this day.

This is just the beginning of the story of how God's love and grace are transforming my heart and life. It would take lots of cups of coffee to tell you the rest, but it's a story I love to tell – especially to others who see themselves as lost causes.

Ask yourself these questions:

What is the story of my journey with God? What is the overarching message or theme? How can I be ready to share my story at the right moment?

Pray this prayer:

Father, thank You for Your loving patience in the writing and re-writing of my life's story. You are the hero in my story, You are the central character. Help me remember all the times and the ways that You have healed me, and changed me. May I see the opportunities You give me to share the story of Your work in my life. And may Your name be glorified in it all. Amen.

Spiritual Disciplines #35

by Tim McGinnin Jr.

"I will lovingly, gently and graciously share with others the story of how God's love and grace has transformed my heart and life."

> *King Agrippa, do you believe the prophets? I know that you believe." And Agrippa said to Paul, "In a short time would you persuade me to be a Christian?" And Paul said, "Whether short or long, I would to God that not only you but also all who hear me this day might become such as I am—except for these chains." (Acts 26:27-29)*

"So, I know I'm supposed to share about Jesus with others. I know I'm supposed to tell people who He is and what He has done. I just have no idea how to do that! Where do I even begin?" Any of those thoughts sound familiar? I can't tell you how many conversations I've had with my brothers and sisters in Christ who have made this kind of statement to me in conversation. I know I personally wrestled with this as a newer believer. The biggest question that comes up doesn't seem to be around what a witness is, so much as it is "how do I share my faith?" and "what kinds of things should I even talk about?"

In Acts 26, during his trial with King Agrippa, the apostle Paul uses a simple approach to sharing his story that we can use as an outline today. There are of course other ways to tackle sharing our story, but this is a great way to start answering the question of "how?"—Paul talks about four primary things:

1. Life before Jesus (26:1-11)
2. How he became a follower of Jesus (26:12-18)
3. How life is different following Jesus (26:19-23)
4. An invitation to follow Jesus (26:26-29)

You'll notice when you read Acts 26, that Paul's account is rather short. He shares his testimony with the King in less than 700 words, which is just under a page typed in 12-point font. I encourage you to take some time and write about each of the four areas in a paragraph each. This will help you to form the basis of what you can share with others when you move forward in the discipline of sharing your story with others. Whether you've shared your story with others thousands of times, or you are wrestling with how to do this for the first time, this simple writing exercise helps us to reflect on the Glory of God in our lives that can be shared with those around us!

Ask yourself these questions:

What was my life like before Jesus? How did I come to the decision to become a follower of Jesus? How is my life different since I began following Jesus? Who is the Lord calling me to share my testimony with?

Pray this prayer:

Lord, thank You for allowing me to have a relationship with You through Jesus Christ. Thank You for the privilege of being called Your beloved child. Give me boldness and clarity in my testimony of faith and encounter with You. Empower me to boldly share my story with gentleness, grace, and love so that others might come to know You and have a story to tell of their own.

Made in United States
North Haven, CT
26 April 2022